The Real Exorcist:

Spiritual Warfare Methodology

Volume Two

Fr. Jack Ashcraft

CHAPTER ONE
THE PSYCHOLOGY OF EXORCISM

For though we walk in the flesh, we do not war after the flesh: For the weapons of our warfare are not carnal, but mighty through God to the pulling down of strong holds; Casting down imaginations, and every high thing that exalteth itself against the knowledge of God, and bringing into captivity every thought to the obedience of Christ.
-II Corinthians 10:3-5

Paul warned the Corinthian church not to be ignorant of Satan's "wiles." the Greek word for wiles means "schemes" and is from the same word used for "mind." Basically, Satan's primary focus of attacks occur in our thought and emotional/mental life. Thus it is no stretch to say that the mind is the central spiritual battlefield. Each and every attack of Satan involves the human mind in some form or fashion. This does not mean that everyone suffering from the various emotional and mental ailments is possessed. The exorcist should NEVER assume such. These are far more often organic issues best dealt with trained medical professionals. However such emotional/mental states can also be indicative of diabolic oppression. Oppression is not the same as possession and should not be treated as such. Oppression is best treated through a combination of medical, psychological, and pastoral counseling working symbiotically to heal the whole person. The battle for the mind is easily summarized scripturally:

For to be carnally minded is death; but to be spiritually minded is life and peace. Because the carnal mind is enmity against God: for it is not subject to the law of God, neither indeed can be. -Romans 8:6-7

Satan wants to make the human mind carnal (sinful, worldly, fleshly). God wants the human mind to be spiritually inclined. The mind is a key element in spiritual life and spiritual warfare. The greatest commandment given to humanity includes loving God with all your mind. This is one of the main reasons why Satan battles for your mind.

Jesus said unto him, Thou shalt love the Lord thy God with all thy heart, and with all thy soul, and with all thy mind; This is the first and great commandment. -Matthew 22:37-38

Satan battles for your mind because it is closely tied spiritually to the spirit and to the essence of who we are.

But those things which proceed out of the mouth come forth from the heart; and they defile the man. For out of the heart proceed evil thoughts... -Matthew 15:18-19

Satan battles so strongly for the mind because the way you think affects the way you act.

For as he thinketh in his heart, so is he...- Proverbs 23:7

Satan knows if he can simply control the human mind, twist the thoughts and pervert the mental life, he can control the victims body, his actions, and, if left unchallenged, a demonic entity can enter into the body and possess the victim. Science demonstrates that the mind is one of the most complex and least understood parts of the human body. Because it is so complex, Satan has many subtle methods of attacking the mind. Though it would be impossible to list them all, the following list summarizes the main strategies of attack Satan uses in the battle for the mind.

1. QUESTION THE AUTHORITY OF GOD- The first temptation of humanity started in the mind. It started with this mind game: Questioning the authority of God. Satan said to Eve, "Yea, hath God said?..." Did God really say that you could not eat of the tree of knowledge of good and evil? Questioning God, His Word and His Church leads to doubt, unbelief, and skepticism.

2. DECEPTION AND SEDUCTION- Deception was also part of the Adversary's strategy. When Satan confronted Eve, he was disguised as a beautiful serpent. Satan uses lies, cults, and "religious spirits" to deceive millions in our world today. Some of the deceptions Satan utilizes include the following lies:

• "You can become a god."
• "You can know the future."
• "You future, including eternity, is predestined. There is nothing you can do about it."
• "Everyone is a child of God."

- "There are more ways to Heaven than by Jesus."
- "God is too good to send anyone to Hell."
- "All God expects you to do is live a good life and do the best you can."
- "The Bible should not be taken literally."
- "The Bible contains many errors."

The lying spirits of Satan attack the mind to confuse you and distort the truth of God's Word.

Now the Spirit speaketh expressly, that in the latter times some shall depart from the faith, giving heed to seducing spirits and doctrines of devils.
-I Timothy 4:1

3. THE FLESH- In volume one of this work we examined the flesh as a potential spiritual force of evil. Demonic entities will use the flesh to attack the mind.

But I see another law in my members, warring against the law of my mind, and bringing me into captivity to the law of sin which is in my members.
-Romans 7:23

The demonic will manipulate speech, sight, sound, and even the senses of touch and smell to foster wicked thoughts in the human mind.

4. DEPRESSION- To be depressed is to be downcast, sad, discouraged, or in a very low spiritual and mental state. It includes feelings of despair, despondency, and dejection. Depression can lead to suicidal thoughts or actual suicide because of the hopeless feelings which

produces uncontrollable mental grief, sorrow, heartache, and crying. Sometimes demons use circumstances of life to lead to depression. For examples, a great loss or fear of loss, suppressed anger, a low self concept, unfulfilled expectations, and a negative attitude can all be used to cause depression. In Proverbs 24:10 we are warned about "fainting in the day of adversity" (troubled or distressed circumstances). Sometimes depression is caused by the negative attitudes of those around us through which Satan works. In Deuteronomy 1:28 God's people admitted, "our brethren have discouraged our hearts." We read in Numbers 21:4 that the soul of God's people was much discouraged. King David often reflected discouragement in his Psalms (see Psalms 69 for an example). The Apostle Paul also had times of deep depression.

For we would not, brethren, have you ignorant of our trouble which came to us in Asia, that we were pressed out of measure, above strength, insomuch that we despaired even of life... -II Corinthians 1:8

If you do not conquer depression it can also lead to oppression by Satanic spirits. This is a deeper form of depression where Satan gains more restrictive power over the mind.

5. DISCOURAGEMENT- Discouragement means to be "without courage." Demonic entities want to discourage you because if you are "without courage," you are ineffective in spiritual warfare.
6. WITHDRAWAL- Another way demons attack the mind is through withdrawal. The purpose of this

strategy is to isolate you from the rest of the Body of Christ. Such withdrawal isoltaes you from the source of sacramental grace, community prayer and healing.

7. NEGATIVE ATTITUDES AND EMOTIONS-Demons cause negative attitudes towards others. They instill envy, jealousy, suspicion, unforgiveness, distrust, anger, hatred, intolerance, prejudice, competition, impatience, judging, criticism, covetousness, and selfishness. They also try to cause greed, discontent, pride, vanity, ego, importance, arrogance, intellectualism, and self-righteousness. These negative outlooks lead to negative emotions and both stem from your thought life. These attitudes and emotions render you ineffective in spiritual warfare.

8. REBELLION- Demons also influence rebellious thoughts. Rebellion is willful disobedience of God's authority and the authority of His Church. Rebellion includes self-will, stubbornness, and disobedience. Remember that rebellion was the original sin of Satan. His five statements of "I will" demonstrated his rebellion (Isaiah 14:12-14). The "I will" spirit is a way to recognize the operation of the demonic through rebellion.

9. ACCUSATION AND CONDEMNATION- Satan is called "the accuser of the brethren" (Revelation 12:10). He influences accusation to enter your mind, makes you feel inferior, and condemns you. He will give you guilty feelings of shame,

unworthiness, and embarrassment.

10. SEXUAL IMPURITY- Demons will insert thoughts of sexual impurity, lust, and mental sexual fantasies. Christ said:

But I say unto you, That whosoever looketh on a woman to lust after her hath committed adultery with her already in his heart. -Matthew 5:28

11. CONFUSION- Demons also cause indecision, confusion, and frustration in your mind. When you are confused, indecisive, and frustrated, you obviously cannot be a strong and powerful witness for Christ.

12. TORMENTING THOUGHTS- Worry, anxiety, dread, apprehension, and nervousness are all used to attack the mind. Mental torment can also come through an overactive mind that will not "shut off" or an under active mind that cannot function properly. Tormenting thoughts also include fear, and bitter memories of events that should be forgiven and forgotten.

13. COMPROMISE- To "compromise" is to settle conflicting principles by adjustment. The principles of God and Satan are in opposition. Satan tries to get you to compromise your spiritual principles. For example, he will tell you it is not necessary to attend the Divine Liturgy each Sunday, to believe the Bible literally, to support the work of the Church, to study the Sacred Scriptures, to pray daily, etc.

MENTAL CONDITIONS

If the demonic is allowed to persist with thoughts of depression, suicide, torment, accusation, etc., it can lead to mental illness. This could include a nervous or mental breakdown and various medically recognized mental conditions. It is essential that investigators and priests have a basic understanding of the types of mental health issues that can be mistaken for demonic activity. The following information is provided purely for informational purposes and not for diagnosis. Investigators and priests are not mental health professionals and are never to diagnose or act as if they are medical or mental health professionals. The fact that someone is suffering from depression or any other mental illness should never be used as a determining factor for demonic activity or to proceed with an exorcism. Nor should an investigator or priest at any time suggest anything resembling demonic imagery.

Temporal Lobe Epilepsy-Temporal lobe epilepsy (TLE) was defined in 1985 by the International League Against Epilepsy (ILAE) as a condition characterized by recurrent unprovoked seizures originating from the medial or lateral temporal lobe. The seizures associated with temporal lobe epilepsy consist of simple partial seizures without loss of awareness and complex partial seizures (ie, with loss of awareness). The individual loses awareness during a complex partial seizure because the seizure spreads to involve both temporal lobes, which causes impairment of memory. The partial seizures may secondarily generalize. Temporal lobe epilepsy was first recognized in 1881 by John Hughlings Jackson, who described "uncinate fits" seizures arising from the uncal part of temporal lobe and the "dreamy state." In the 1940s, Gibbs et al introduced the term *psychomotor epilepsy*. The international classification of epileptic seizures (1981) replaced the term *psychomotor seizures* with *complex partial seizures*. The ILAE classification of the epilepsies uses the term *temporal lobe epilepsy* and divides the etiologies into cryptogenic (presumed unidentified etiology), idiopathic (genetic), and symptomatic (cause known, eg, tumor). Although the causes of temporal lobe epilepsy are widely varied, hippocampal sclerosis is the most common pathologic finding. Hippocampal sclerosis involves hippocampal cell loss in the CA1 and CA3 regions and the dentate hilus. The CA2 region is relatively spared. The clinical correlate on neuroimaging on MRI is called mesial temporal lobe sclerosis.Approximately 50% of patients with epilepsy have partial epilepsy. Partial epilepsy is often of temporal lobe origin. However, the true prevalence of temporal lobe epilepsy is not known, since not all cases of presumed temporal lobe epilepsy are confirmed by video-EEG and most cases are classified by clinical history and interictal EEG findings alone. The temporal lobe is the most epileptogenic region of the brain. In fact, 90% of patients with temporal interictal epileptiform abnormalities on their EEG have a history of seizures. Temporal lobe epilepsy is not more common in one sex but female patients may experience catamenial epilepsy, which is an increase of seizures during the menstrual period. Epilepsy occurs in all age groups, but a group where it was underrecognized is in elderly persons. Epilepsy in elderly persons may not be as dramatic and often may present as confusion or memory lapses. The index for suspicion should be low as patients are often misdiagnosed and not treated appropriately.

- Aura
    - Auras occur in approximately 80% of temporal lobe seizures. They are a common feature of simple partial seizures and usually precede complex partial seizures of temporal lobe origin.
    - Auras may be classified by symptom type; the types comprise somatosensory, special sensory, autonomic, or psychic symptoms.
- Somatosensory and special sensory phenomena
    - Olfactory and gustatory illusions and hallucinations may occur. Acharya et al found that olfactory auras are more commonly associated with temporal lobe tumors than with other causes of temporal lobe epilepsy.
    - Auditory hallucinations consist of a buzzing sound, a voice or voices, or muffling of ambient sounds. This type of aura is more common with neocortical temporal lobe epilepsy than with other types of temporal lobe epilepsy.
    - Patients may report distortions of shape, size, and distance of objects.
    - These visual illusions are unlike the visual hallucinations associated with occipital lobe seizure in that no formed elementary visual image is noted, such as the visual image of a face that may be seen with seizures arising from the fusiform or the inferior

temporal gyrus.
- Things may appear shrunken (micropsia) or larger (macropsia) than usual.
- Tilting of structures has been reported. Vertigo has been described with seizures in the posterior superior temporal gyrus.
- Psychic phenomena
  - Patients may have a feeling of déjà vu or jamais vu, a sense of familiarity or unfamiliarity, respectively.
  - Patients may experience depersonalization (ie, feeling of detachment from oneself) or derealization (ie, surroundings appear unreal).
  - Fear or anxiety usually is associated with seizures arising from the amygdala. Sometimes, the fear is strong, described as an "impending sense of doom."
  - Patients may describe a sense of dissociation or autoscopy, in which they report seeing their own body from outside.
- Autonomic phenomena are characterized by changes in heart rate, piloerection, and sweating. Patients may experience an epigastric "rising" sensation or nausea.

Physical

- Following the aura, a temporal lobe complex partial seizure begins with a wide-eyed, motionless stare, dilated pupils, and behavioral arrest. Oral alimentary automatisms such as lip smacking, chewing, and swallowing may be noted. Manual automatisms or unilateral dystonic posturing of a limb also may be observed.

- Patients may continue their ongoing motor activity or react to their surroundings in a semipurposeful manner (ie, reactive automatisms). They can have repetitive stereotyped manual automatisms.

- A complex partial seizure may evolve to a secondarily generalized tonic-clonic seizure. Often, the documentation of a seizure only notes the generalized tonic-clonic component of the seizure. A careful history from the patient or an observer is needed to elicit the partial features of either a simple seizure or a complex partial seizure before the secondarily generalized seizure is important.

- Patients usually experience a postictal period of confusion, which distinguishes temporal lobe epilepsy from absence seizures, which are not associated with postictal confusion. In addition, absence seizures are not associated with auras nor with complex automatisms. Postictal aphasia suggests onset in the language-dominant temporal lobe.

- Most auras and automatisms last a very short period—seconds or 1-2 minutes. The postictal phase may last for a longer period (several minutes). By definition, amnesia occurs during a complex partial seizure because of bilateral hemispheric involvement.

Causes

- Approximately two thirds of patients with temporal lobe epilepsy treated surgically have hippocampal sclerosis as the pathologic substrate.
- The etiologies of temporal lobe epilepsy include the following:
    - Infections, eg, herpes encephalitis, bacterial meningitis, neurocysticercosis
    - Trauma producing contusion or hemorrhage that results in encephalomalacia or cortical scarring; difficult traumatic delivery such as forceps deliveries
    - Hamartomas
    - Malignancies (eg, meningiomas, gliomas, gangliomas)
    - Vascular malformations (ie, arteriovenous malformation, cavernous angioma)
    - Cryptogenic: A cause is presumed but has not been identified.
    - Idiopathic (genetic): This is rare. Familial temporal lobe epilepsy was described by Berkovic and colleagues, and partial epilepsy with auditory features was described by Scheffer and colleagues.
- Hippocampal sclerosis produces a clinical syndrome called mesial temporal lobe epilepsy (MTLE).
- Febrile seizures: The association of simple febrile seizure with temporal lobe epilepsy has been controversial. However, a subset of children with complex febrile convulsions appear to be at risk of developing temporal lobe epilepsy in later life.

Complex febrile seizures are febrile seizures that last longer than 15 minutes, have focal features, or recur within 24 hours.

Schizophrenia-Schizophrenia is a mental disorder that makes it difficult to tell the difference between real and unreal experiences, to think logically, to have normal emotional responses, and to behave normally in social situations. Schizophrenia is a complex illness. Even experts in the field are not sure what causes it. Some doctors think that the brain may not be able to process information correctly. Genetic factors appear to play a role.People who have family members with schizophrenia may be more likely to get the disease themselves. Some researchers believe that events in a person's environment may trigger schizophrenia. For example, problems (infection) during development in the mother's womb and at birth may increase the risk for developing schizophrenia later in life. Psychological and social factors may also affect its development. However, the level of social and family support appears to affect the course of illness and may protect against the condition returning.
There are 5 types of schizophrenia:

- Catatonic
- Disorganized
- Paranoid
- Residual
- Undifferentiated

Schizophrenia usually begins before the age of 45,

symptoms last for 6 months or more, and people start to lose their ability to socialize and work. Schizophrenia is thought to affect about 1% of people worldwide. Schizophrenia appears to occur in equal rates among men and women, but in women it begins later. For this reason, males tend to account for more than half of patients in services with high numbers of young adults. Although schizophrenia usually begins in young adulthood, there are cases in which the disorder begins later (over 45 years).

Childhood-onset schizophrenia begins after the age of 5 and, in most cases, after normal development. Childhood schizophrenia is rare and can be difficult to tell apart from other developmental disorders of childhood, such as autism. Schizophrenia may have a variety of symptoms. Usually the illness develops slowly over months or even years.

At first, the symptoms may not be noticeable. For example, you may feel tense, or have trouble sleeping or concentrating. You can become isolated and withdrawn, and have trouble making or keeping friends.

As the illness continues, symptoms develop:

- An appearance or mood that shows no emotion (flat affect)
- Bizarre motor behavior in which there is less reaction to the environment (catatonic behavior)
- False beliefs or thoughts that have nothing to do with reality (delusions)
- Hearing, seeing, or feeling things that are not

there (hallucinations)
- Thoughts "jump" between unrelated topics (disordered thinking)

Symptoms can be different depending on the type of schizophrenia.

Catatonic type:

- Agitation
- Decreased sensitivity to pain
- Inability to take care of personal needs
- Negative feelings
- Motor disturbances
- Rigid muscles
- Stupor

Paranoid type:

- Anger
- Anxiety
- Argumentativeness
- Delusions of persecution or grandeur

Disorganized type:

- Child-like (regressive) behavior
- Delusions
- Flat affect
- Hallucinations
- Inappropriate laughter
- Not understandable (incoherence)

- Repetitive behaviors
- Social withdrawal

Undifferentiated type may include symptoms of more than one type of schizophrenia.

Residual type -- symptoms of the illness have gone away, but some features, such as hallucinations and flat affect, may remain.

Dissociative Identity Disorder-Dissociative identity disorder (previously known as multiple personality disorder) is a fairly common effect of severe trauma during early childhood, usually extreme, repetitive physical, sexual, and/or emotional abuse. Most of us have experienced mild dissociation, which is like daydreaming or getting lost in the moment while working on a project. However, dissociative identity disorder is a severe form of dissociation, a mental process, which produces a lack of connection in a person's thoughts, memories, feelings, actions, or sense of identity. Dissociative identity disorder is thought to stem from trauma experienced by the person with the disorder. The dissociative aspect is thought to be a coping mechanism -- the person literally dissociates himself from a situation or experience that's too violent, traumatic, or painful to assimilate with his conscious self. Dissociative identity disorder is characterized by the presence of two or more distinct or split identities or personality states that continually have power over the person's behavior. With dissociative identity disorder, there's also an inability to recall key personal information that is too far-reaching to be explained as mere forgetfulness. With dissociative identity disorder, there are also highly distinct memory variations, which fluctuate with the person's split personality.

The "alters" or different identities have their own age, sex, or race. Each has his or her own postures, gestures, and distinct way of talking. Sometimes the alters are imaginary people; sometimes they are animals. As each personality reveals itself and controls the individuals' behavior and thoughts, it's called "switching." Switching can take seconds to minutes to days. When under hypnosis, the person's different "alters" or identities may be very responsive to the therapist's requests.Along with the dissociation and multiple or split personalities, people with dissociative disorders may experience any of the following symptoms:

- Depression
- Mood swings
- Suicidal tendencies
- Sleep disorders (insomnia, night terrors)
- Anxiety and phobias (flashbacks, reactions to stimuli or "triggers")
- Alcohol and drug abuse
- Compulsions and rituals
- Psychotic-like symptoms (including auditory and visual hallucinations)
- Eating disorders

Other symptoms of dissociative identity disorder may include headache, amnesia, time loss, trances, and "out of body experiences." Some people with dissociative disorders have a tendency toward self-persecution, self-sabotage, and even violence (both self-inflicted and outwardly directed). As an example, someone with dissociative identity disorder may find themselves doing things they wouldn't normally do such as speeding, reckless driving, or stealing money from their employer or friend, yet they feel they are being compelled to do it. Some describe this feeling as being a passenger in their body rather than the driver. In other words, they truly believe they have no choice.

There are several main ways in which the psychological processes of dissociative identity disorder change the way a person experiences living, including the following:

- **Depersonalization.** This is a sense of being detached from one's body and is often referred to as an "out-of-body" experience.
- **Derealization.** This is the feeling that the world is not real or looking foggy or far away.
- **Amnesia.** This is the failure to recall significant personal information that is so extensive it cannot be blamed on ordinary forgetfulness. There can also be micro-amnesias where the discussion engaged in is not remembered, or the content of a meaningful conversation is forgotten from one second to the next.
- **Identity confusion** or **identity alteration.** Both of these involve a sense of confusion about who a person is. An example of identity confusion is when a person sometimes feels a thrill while engaged in an activity (such as reckless driving, DUI, alcohol or drug abuse) which at other times would be revolting. In addition to these apparent alterations, the person may experience distortions

in time, place, and situation.

It is now acknowledged that these dissociated states are not fully-mature personalities, but rather they represent a disjointed sense of identity. With the amnesia typically associated with dissociative identity disorder, different identity states remember different aspects of autobiographical information. There is usually a host personality within the individual, who identifies with the person's real name. Ironically, the host personality is usually unaware of the presence of other personalities.

The distinct personalities may serve diverse roles in helping the individual cope with life's dilemmas. For instance, there's an average of two to four personalities present when the patient is initially diagnosed. Then there's an average of 13 to 15 personalities that can become known over the course of treatment. While unusual, there have been instances of dissociative identity disorder with more than 100 personalities. Environmental triggers or life events cause a sudden shift from one alter or personality to another. While the causes of dissociative identity disorder are still vague, research indicates that a combination of environmental and biological factors work together to cause it. As many as 98% to 99% of individuals who develop dissociative disorders have recognized personal histories of recurring, overpowering, and often life-threatening disturbances at a sensitive developmental stage of childhood (usually before age 9). Dissociation may also happen when there has been insistent neglect or emotional abuse, even when there has been no overt physical or sexual abuse. Findings show that in families where parents are frightening and unpredictable, the children may become dissociative. Statistics show the rate of dissociative identity disorder is .01% to 1% of the general population. Still, more than 1/3 of people say they feel as if they're watching themselves in a movie at times, and 7% percent of the population may have undiagnosed dissociative disorder.

The point of examining such mental health issues is to demonstrate the very serious need for investigators and priests to be absolutely certain that the client has undergone a complete mental health evaluation and is not diagnosed with or being treated for any mental health issues. If indeed the client is, the priest should proceed with pastoral counseling under the guidance of the clients mental health professional.

Notes:

1. In the battle for the mind, Satan tries attempts to cause:
- A carnal mind: Romans 8:6-7
- A mind alienated from God by wicked works: Colossians 1:21
- A defiled mind: Titus 1:15
- A fleshly mind: Ephesians 2:3
- A hardened mind: Daniel 5:20
- A doubtful mind: Luke 12:29
- A vain mind: Ephesians 4:17
- A blinded mind: II Corinthians 3:14
- A seared mind and conscience: Titus 1:15
- A despiteful mind: Ezekiel 36:5
- An evil mind: Acts 14:2
- An unbelieving mind: II Corinthians 4:4
- A fainting mind: Hebrews 12:3
- A reprobate mind: II Timothy 3:8
- Double mindedness: James 1:8; 4:8
- A corrupt mind: I Timothy 6:5; II Timothy 3:8; II Corinthians 11:3

2. Positive mental qualities you should develop:
- A ready mind: II Corinthians 8:19; I Peter 5:2; Acts 17:11
- A pure mind: II Peter 3:1
- A stayed mind: Isaiah 26:3
- A renewed mind: Ephesians 4:23; Romans 12:2
- A humble mind: Colossians 3:12; Acts 20:19
- A sober mind: Titus 2:6
- A sound mind: II Timothy 1:7
- A mind of love: Matthew 22:37
- A serving mind: Romans 7:25
- A fully persuaded mind: Romans 14:5

• A fervent mind: II Corinthians 7:7
• A willing mind: II Corinthians 8:12
3. Because of continued sin, men can be turned over to a reprobate mind. See Romans 1:28- 32. A reprobate mind is the most evil kind of mind you can imagine.
4. As you learned in this chapter, one of the strategies for victory in the mind is to let the same mind that was in Jesus be in you. Study the New Testament further to discover just what the mind of Jesus was like. What mental attitudes were reflected in His actions? How did His ministry reflect His thought life? How did His words reflect His thoughts?

   5. Jesus knows even the thoughts of your mind: See Luke 5:22; 6:8; 11:17.

CHAPTER TWO
PHYSICAL ATTACKS

The thief cometh not, but for to steal, and to kill, and to destroy: I am come that they might have life, and that they might have it more abundantly.
-John 10:10

The body of the Christian is a temple of the Holy Spirit.

Know ye not that ye are the temple of God, and that the Spirit of God dwelleth in you? If any man defile the temple of God, him shall God destroy; for the temple of God is holy, which temple ye are.
-I Corinthians 3:16-17

Because the body of the Christian is a temple of the Holy Spirit, and because we were created in God's Image, it is often attacked by demonic entities through various means.

ILLNESS- Illness exists because of the original sin of Adam and Eve. Although all illness is in the world because of sin, it does not mean everyone who is suffering is doing so because of personal sins. Sacred Scripture reveals various reasons for illness. The first is illness caused by the demonic. Demons attempt to afflict the body just as they attempt to afflict the spirit. The body is no more immune to attack than the spirit is to discouragement, condemnation, etc. But illness can also be used as a way for God to deal with personal sin. For an example see the story of Miriam in Numbers 12. In one healing Christ performed during His earthly ministry He said to the person:

...Behold, thou art made whole: sin no more, lest a worse thing come unto thee. -John 5:14

The illness of this man was apparently a result of sin. In another case, Christ made it clear that the illness was not the result of sin but for the glory of God:

And as Jesus passed by, He saw a man which was blind from his birth. And His disciples asked Him, saying, Master, who did sin, this man, or his parents, that he was born blind? Jesus answered, Neither hath this man sinned, nor his parents; but that the works of God should be made manifest in him. -John 9:1-3

An illness for the glory of God is one which God allows for His glory when physical healing comes through prayer. There have also been cases of possession and oppression where this has been true. All illness however is not caused by sin, the demonic or as a chastisement. Illness is far more often the result of natural laws. For example, you may become ill because you do not eat properly.

EXTREME FATIGUE- Demons will also attack the body through fatigue which results from being too busy or overworked. When a client is extremely tired physically, demons may take advantage and spiritually assault the victim. Satan came to Christ when He was exhausted from 40 days of fasting (Matthew 4:2). When Elijah was tired from great spiritual exploits he became so discouraged that he wanted to die (I Kings 19:4).

DEATH- Although physical death is a part of the natural scheme of human life until the return of Christ, demonic entities will attempt to cause premature death. They often tempt their victims to commit suicide.

ABUSE- Demonic entities also encourage their victims to abuse their bodies by putting toxic substances into them such as drugs and alcoholic beverages, or in cutting, piercing and scratching their bodies.

In regards to physical attacks caused by demonic entities it is important that the priest counsel the client that the client that as a Christian, God is in control of their life and the Holy Spirit a protective covering over them. Demons cannot harm them nor take their life without the knowledge of God. The power of Christ the King is greater than that of Satan. The God who made the human body has the power to heal that body.

But unto you that fear my name, shall the Sun of righteousness arise with healing in His wings...
-Malachi 4:2

Who His own self bare our sins in His own body on the tree, that we, being dead to sins should live unto righteousness; by whose stripes ye were healed.
-I Peter 2:24

But He was wounded for our transgressions, He was bruised for our iniquities; the chastisement of our peace was upon Him, and with His stripes we are healed. -Isaiah 53:5

Beloved, I wish above all things that thou mayest prosper and be in health, even as thy soul prospereth. -III John 1:2

Often when a demon attacks a client physically, this can be a sign of oppression. The priest and intercessors should pray for the client and family, bless the home and arrange for long term pastoral counseling.

Is any sick among you? Let him call for the elders of the church; and let them pray over him, anointing him with oil in the name of the Lord: And the prayer of faith shall save the sick, and the Lord shall raise him up; and if he have committed sins, they shall be forgiven him. -James 5:14-15

In addition, the priest and lay investigator may witness such physical abuse against the victim (and sometimes the exorcist) as:

- Scratches and claw marks
- Words scratched into the flesh
- Shoving and pushing
- Spontaneous bruising
- Contortion of limbs and soft flesh areas
- Lifting of the body

- Throwing of the body
- Burning sensations often accompanied by red marks
- Violent itching and rashing
- Vomiting profusely (sometimes objects)

And there are many more physical manifestations of this sort. This is by no means an exhaustive list, but merely designed to give the reader a basic idea of the scope of activity to be expected.

ATTACKS ON THE FAMILY

The family is the basic unit of society established by God in the beginning of the world when He first created man. God has always emphasized the family and it is a divine institution. The Almighty raised up a nation of chosen people from the family of one man, Abraham. He selected the physical union of a man and his wife to describe the spiritual union between Christ and the Church. Throughout the Scriptures, God stressed the importance of the family in His will for humanity. Because of the importance of the family in society, the family is a primary target for attack by the demonic forces. Demons undermine the union between a man and his wife in Holy Matrimony. Demons influence people to engage in improper sexual relationships which result in grave mortal sin (I Corinthians 7:5). They are behind the sin of adultery (Galatians 5:19). The spiritual forces of Satan destroy and divide the home. This can range from arguments through divorce and even into legislation and laws which undermine the family unit.

...Every kingdom divided against itself is brought to desolation; and every city or house divided against itself shall not stand. -Matthew 12:25

Once the demonic forces establish division and destroy the homes of a nation, they can gradually erode and undermine the entire nation itself. (This is a good point to keep in mind. Every spiritual battle is connected to a greater spiritual goal.) God established a chain of command in the home. The man is to be the head of the home and love his wife. The wife is to follow his leadership and the children are to be in submission to their parents (I Corinthians 7; Ephesians 5:1-6:1). Demonic forces often attack the man of the home and tempt him to act in unloving or even abusive ways. This results in a loss of respect, trust and obedience from the wife and children. The demons then tempt the wife to act in rebellion against the husband. Demons will also target the children. They will create an atmosphere of lack of discipline which results in rebellion. Read the story of Eli's sons in I Samuel 2 and of David's son, Absalom, in II Samuel 13-19. When a family unit is composed of Christians and unbelievers, spiritual division exists. This division is not a conflict between flesh and blood. It is a spiritual conflict. It cannot be won by harsh words or through debate and argument. The forces of hell fight the unity of the family because it is a natural parallel of the unity between Christ and His Church. Christian families must recognize this and declare with Sacred Scripture:

...but as for me and my house, we will serve the Lord. -Joshua 24:15

The priest and investigator should be careful to observe the family dynamic. How do they interact? Do they eat meals together? Pray together? Take recreation together? Is there an abnormal amount of familial bickering and argumentation? Is there a member of the family who is not a Christian? In some cases of oppression and possession the demonic entity will manifest to other family members, cause objects to fly at them, frighten them with sounds, foul odours, etc. Be certain to interview each family member separately, and then the family together as a unit. Pay attention to any apparent inconsistencies as these may be indicative of demonic doorways that allow the oppression to continue.

Notes:
1. Read the book of Job. Job was attacked in the physical, material, and family realms. He was also attacked through human personalities. Behind each of these circumstances and areas of attack there was a spiritual reason. See Job.1:6-12; 2:1-6; 42:5.

CHAPTER THREE
TRANSFERENCE OF SPIRITS

**And I will come down and talk with thee there: and I will take of the spirit which is upon thee, and will put it upon them; and they shall bear the burden of the people with thee, that thou bear it not thyself alone.
-Numbers 11:17**

Your youngest son was raised to be part of a closely knit family with good communication. He respected your rules and you attended church together. Suddenly he does not want to be with the family or attend church. He becomes sullen, withdrawn, and rebellious. He defies your instructions and stays out late at night. You cannot understand the sudden change. You did not have this problem with your older son. You have given them both the same love and guidance. What caused this situation?

Examine the problem with your son and you will find the change came about after someone else came into his life who he respected and admired. He began to associate closely with this person. He began to tell you what they thought or said and what their parents allowed and he began to pattern himself after their style of behavior and dress. His spiritual covering was removed (your guidance) and demonic entities were allowed to oppress him.

TRANSFERENCE OF SPIRITS
Situations like this are called "transference of spirits." To "transfer" means to convey from one person to another. The word "spirit" as used here refers to the

"character, attitude, or motive behind an action," not the demon itself. (Transference of spirits can be a generational plaguing by a demonic entity as well.) The actions of each person exhibit a certain "spirit." For example, a person can demonstrate a gentle spirit, a boisterous spirit, or a rebellious spirit by his actions. A person's spirit can be influenced by the spiritual forces of good or evil and he can transfer his spirit to others on a personal or group basis. This transference of spirits accounts for many of the spiritual battles fought by priests in this area of ministry. It accounts for the abrupt changes from positive to negative behavior which we witness in those around us. It explains why two children, raised in the same home, who receive the same Christian training, can turn out so differently. It is the reason behind divisions in homes, friendships, and the Church. When you maintain close association with or come under the influence of a person with a spirit more powerful than yours, you are open to the transference of that spirit to your own spirit. You are influenced by that spirit and it is transferred to you. Even more alarmingly, the demonic entity behind the spirit may attach itself to the client and continue to oppress him and even his family for generations to come. This is why we hear of cases in paranormal research wherein the family has had a "ghost", so they think, that has haunted their family for generations. This is in fact a demonic entity attached through transference of spirits. This attachment is made stronger when the family unit, or a femaily member, exhibits the characteristics that caused the original attachment. In cases such as this the priest will need to bless the home and property, and will arrange long term pastoral counseling with the family. The family must be willing to join together as a unit and do whatever necessary to end the generational transference, otherwise no blessings will stop the situation.

The book of Proverbs warns repeatedly of the danger of association with those who have wrong spirits. For examples read Proverbs 1:10-19 and 2:11-22. We are warned:

Make no friendship with an angry man; and with a furious man thou shalt not go; Lest thou learn his ways, and get a snare to thy soul. -Proverbs 22:24-25

Enter not into the path of the wicked, and go not in the way of evil men. Avoid it, pass not by it, turn from it, and pass away. -Proverbs 4:14-15

Go from the presence of a foolish man, when thou perceivest not in him the lips of knowledge. -Proverbs 14:7

Clients should be counseled to choose close associates carefully. Parents should carefully monitor the associates of their children.

Notes:

1. Study further the transference of a good spirit: The prophet Elisha asked for the "mantle" of Elijah to fall upon him at the time of Elijah's death. This "mantle" symbolized the spirit of God which was upon Elijah. Elisha asked for a "double portion" of the good spirit which rested on Elijah. Read the story in II Kings 2.

2. Study further the transference of an evil spirit: Read the story of Ananias and Sapphira in Acts 5:1-11. This is an example of a husband who transferred a spirit of deception to his wife.

3. Study the following references. They reveal the many ways your spirit can be affected with certain attitudes and emotional responses, both right and wrong. Your spirit can be:

Jealous: Numbers 5:14
Hardened: Deuteronomy 2;30
In Anguish: Exodus 6:9
Good: Nehemiah 9:20
Guileless: Psalms 32:2
Right: Psalms 51:10
Broken: Psalms 51:17
Overwhelmed: Psalms 77:3; 142:3; 143:4
Diligent and searching: Psalms 77:6
Steadfast: Psalms 78:8
Failing within: Psalms 143:7
Faithful: Proverbs 11:13; II Corinthians 4:13
Hasty: Proverbs 14:29; Ecclesiastes 7:9
Haughty: Proverbs 16:18
Humble: Proverbs 16:19
Wounded: Proverbs 18:14
Vexed: Ecclesiastes 1:14
Patient: Ecclesiastes 7:8

Proud: Ecclesiastes 7:8
Seeking: Isaiah 26:9
Judgmental: Isaiah 28:6
In error: Isaiah 29:24
Humble and contrite: Isaiah 57:15
Poor and contrite: Isaiah 66:2
Quieted: Zechariah 6:8
Excellent: Daniel 5:12; 6:3
Grieved: Daniel 7:15
Wise: Exodus 28:3
Strong: Luke 2:40
Wrong: Luke 9:55
Worshipful: John 4:23-24; Philippians 3:3
Troubled: Genesis 41:8; Daniel 2:3; John 13:21; II Thessalonians 2:2
Persuasive: Acts 6:10
Stirred: Ezra 1:1; Haggai 1:14; Acts 7:16
Pressed: Acts 18:5
Fervent: Acts 18:25; Romans 12:11
Bound: Acts 20:22
Serving: Romans 1:9
Circumcised: Romans 2:29
New: Ezekiel 11:19;18:31; 36:26; Romans 7:6
In bondage: Romans 8:15
Bear witness with God's spirit: Romans 8:16
Slumbering: Romans 11:8
Meek: Galatians 6:1
Meek and quiet: I Peter 3:4
Prayerful: I Corinthians 14:14;
One with God: I Corinthians 6:17
Glorifying God: I Corinthians 6:20
Singing: I Corinthians 14:15
Refreshed: I Corinthians 16:18; II Corinthians 7:13

Restless: II Corinthians 2:13
Filthy: II Corinthians 7:1
United with other believers: II Corinthians 12:18;
Philippians 1:27
Preserved: I Thessalonians 5:23
An example of the believers: I Timothy 4:12
Fearful: II Timothy 1:7
Lustful: James 4:5
Willing: Exodus 35:21; Matthew 26:41
Poor: Matthew 5:3
Perceptive: Mark 2:8
Ready: Mark 14:38
Sorrowful: I Samuel 1:15
Sad: I Kings 21:5
Rejoicing: Luke 1:47
Sighing: Mark 8:12
4. Do you feel you have been affected by the transference of a demonic entity? Who do you believe influenced your spirit? What were the results of this negative influence? If you have been affected by the transference of an evil spirit and to defend against being affected by such, follow these spiritual strategies:
• Control your own spirit.
• Guard your tongue.
• Guard your affections.
• Carefully select your associates.
• Guard your physical senses.

CHAPTER FOUR
CULTS AND THE OCCULT

In the investigation process of demonic claims it is not infrequent to come into contact with individuals involved in a variety of religious cults and/or the occult. It is important for both the lay investigator and priest to be aware of some basics regarding this area of investigation.Lets start by answering some basic questions.

Dont cultists wear weird clothing and live in communes?

While it is true that some cults do require communal living and adopting different clothing and dietary habits, many are nearly undetectable. Cults are becoming more sophisticated in their approach, and so dress, talk and act in ways that allow them to assimilate easily while subtly promoting their teachings. One cult has even invented a phrase to describe this, they call it "being relatable".

Aren't most cult members mentally ill?

Absolutely not. Many cult members are very intelligent, educated, sharp minded and skilled. The reality is that all sorts of people are involved in cults. The usual way in which they are attracted to a cult is through contact during a crisis period of their personal life.

Types of Cults

Religious

Cults that maintain a religious belief system as their base are the most common. Their belief system could be standard Christianity, Hinduism, Islam or any other of the world religions, or they may have invented their own belief system. What makes them a cult is the fact that they use techniques of mind control to modify the behavior and thinking of cult members, not what they believe.

Business
Cults that use commercial gain as their base are called "cults of greed". They will promise their special programme will help you become very wealthy. Often they will hold up their leader as an example and explain that if you do what he or she says then you will be successful too. Business cults use mind control to get you working for them for free, and to sell you motivational tapes, videos, books and seminars all of which are supposedly designed to help you succeed, but in reality are designed to enhance the cult's mind control environment and keep you believing in their almost impossible dream of success. Of course they never mention that the primary way the leaders make money are by selling these motivation materials to their group!

Self Help Cults
Cults that use "self help" or counselling or self improvement as their base often target business people and corporations. By doing their courses and seminars they claim you and your staff will become more successful. Business people locked away in hotel rooms are subjected to quasi-religious indoctrination as they play strange games, join in group activities, and share their innermost thoughts with the group. Once you have completed one course you are told you need to do the

more advanced course, which naturally costs more than the last. These cults will sometimes request that you do volunteer work and that you help recruit your friends, family and work mates. These groups specialize in creating powerful emotional experiences which are then used to validate your involvement in the cult. The religious overtones are couched in terms which don't sound religious. They usually come to the surface as you near the end of a seminar and are typically New Age oriented.

Political

Cults that use political ideals as their base are well known throughout history. The National Socialist Party, Communist Party, and various racially oriented and nationalistic oriented groups are examples of mind control on a very large scale. On smaller scales white and black supremacists, terrorists, and rebel groups commonly use forms of mind control to recruit and dominate their members.

The Occult

It is also not infrequent for investigators and priests to encounter the occult. The most common forms encountered are:

Wicca- Wicca is an eclectic occult belief system centering around gods, goddesses, and nature worship. Gary Cantrell, a Wiccan author says Wicca is based on "harmony with nature and all aspects of the god and goddess divinity." Wiccan practice involves the manipulation of nature through various rituals in attempts to gain power, prestige, love, or whatever it is a Wiccan seeks. Wicca utilizes symbols in its ceremonies and follows various pagan calendars in reference to Wiccan festivals. Its roots are in ancient agrarian Celtic Society. Wicca does not have a structure of clergy and/or congregations in the sense that Christians understand the terms. It does have priests and priestesses which are in leadership positions within covens that have witches. The varying traditions of Wicca have different requirements for attaining the level of priest and priestess. Some of the more common varieties of Wicca are 1734, Alexandrian, Celtic, Dianic, Dicordian, Eclectic, Gardnerian, and Georgian. Wicca is a recognized as a religion in the military. Some Wiccans practice their rituals "skyclad" (nude). One of the most common aspects of Wiccan belief is the teaching of reincarnation and karma.The purpose of reincarnation is to learn lessons through the various lives. "This process of reincarnation is repeated for numerous lifetimes until a development of the Spirit is reached where the Spirit can truly merge with the male and female balanced creator/creatrix entity. We are returned to the God and to the Goddess." Karma is the law of cause and effect that "does not punish nor reward. It is simply a universal law that reacts to causation until disharmony is illuminated."

Wicca does not claim to be the only way but says that all spiritual traditions and paths are valid to those who practice them. It accepts "the fact that all life is sacred, including plant, animal, and human."

Generally, Wiccans do not believe in the existence of Satan and should not be confused with Satanists.They have no orgies or public displays of sexuality in their rituals, no bestiality, and no blood sacrifices.They do not practice spells with the intention to harm people. They deny that there are moral absolutes, believe that nature is divine, and seek to be in harmony with the earth/nature.

Satanism-Satanism has been around in one form or another for as long as Satan has had direct influence in the lives of the rebellious. The modern expressions of Satanism are quite diverse, ranging from philosophical (denying a literal Satan), to religious (accepting the literal Satan as their god). The oldest of the modern organizations is the Church of Satan, founded by Anton LaVey in 1969. The following beliefs are taken from this particular organization.

The Nine Satanic Statements

1. Satan represents indulgence instead of abstinence!

2. Satan represents vital existence instead of spiritual pipe dreams!

3. Satan represents undefiled wisdom instead of hypocritical self-deceit!

4. Satan represents kindness to those who deserve it instead of love wasted on ingrates!

5. Satan represents vengeance instead of turning the other cheek!

6. Satan represents responsibility to the responsible instead of concern for psychic vampires!

7. Satan represents man as just another animal, sometimes better, more often worse than those that walk on all-fours, who, because of his "divine spiritual and intellectual development," has become the most vicious animal of all!

8. Satan represents all of the so-called sins, as they all lead to physical, mental, or emotional gratification!

9. Satan has been the best friend the Church has ever had, as He has kept it in business all these years! (From the Satanic Bible)

The Eleven Satanic Rules of the Earth

1. Do not give opinions or advice unless you are asked.

2. Do not tell your troubles to others unless you are sure they want to hear them.

3. When in another's lair, show him respect or else do not go there.

4. If a guest in your lair annoys you, treat him cruelly and without mercy.

5. Do not make sexual advances unless you are given the mating signal.

6. Do not take that which does not belong to you unless it is a burden to the other person and he cries out to be relieved.

7. Acknowledge the power of magic if you have employed it successfully to obtain your desires. If you deny the power of magic after having called upon it with success, you will lose all you have obtained.

8. Do not complain about anything to which you need not subject yourself.

9. Do not harm little children.

10. Do not kill non-human animals unless you are attacked or for your food.

11. When walking in open territory, bother no one. If someone bothers you, ask him to stop. If he does not stop, destroy him.

The Nine Satanic Sins

1. Stupidity—The top of the list for Satanic Sins. The Cardinal Sin of Satanism. It's too bad that stupidity isn't painful. Ignorance is one thing, but our society thrives increasingly on stupidity. It depends on people going along with whatever they are told. The media promotes a cultivated stupidity as a posture that is not only acceptable but laudable. Satanists must learn to see through the tricks and cannot afford to be stupid.

2. Pretentiousness—Empty posturing can be most irritating and isn't applying the cardinal rules of Lesser Magic. On equal footing with stupidity for what keeps the money in circulation these days. Everyone's made to feel like a big shot, whether they can come up with the goods or not.

3. Solipsism—Can be very dangerous for Satanists. Projecting your reactions, responses and sensibilities onto someone who is probably far less attuned than you are. It is the mistake of expecting people to give you the same consideration, courtesy and respect that you naturally give them. They won't. Instead, Satanists must strive to apply the dictum of "Do unto others as they do unto you." It's work for most of us and requires constant vigilance lest you slip into a comfortable illusion of everyone being like you. As has been said, certain utopias would be ideal in a nation of philosophers, but unfortunately (or perhaps fortunately, from a Machiavellian standpoint) we are far from that point.

4. Self-deceit—It's in the "Nine Satanic Statements" but deserves to be repeated here. Another cardinal sin. We must not pay homage to any of the sacred cows presented to us, including the roles we are expected to play ourselves. The only time self-deceit should be entered into is when it's fun, and with awareness. But then, it's not self-deceit!

5. Herd Conformity—That's obvious from a Satanic stance. It's all right to conform to a person's wishes, if it ultimately benefits you. But only fools follow along with the herd, letting an impersonal entity dictate to you. The key is to choose a master wisely instead of being enslaved by the whims of the many.

6. Lack of Perspective—Again, this one can lead to a lot of pain for a Satanist. You must never lose sight of who and what you are, and what a threat you can be, by your very existence. We are making history right now, every day. Always keep the wider historical and social picture in mind. That is an important key to both Lesser and Greater Magic. See the patterns and fit things together as you want the pieces to fall into place. Do not be swayed by herd constraints—know that you are working on another level entirely from the rest of the world.

7. Forgetfulness of Past Orthodoxies—Be aware that this is one of the keys to brainwashing people into accepting something new and different, when in reality it's something that was once widely accepted but is now presented in a new package. We are expected to rave about the genius of the creator and forget the original. This makes for a disposable society.

8. Counterproductive Pride—That first word is important. Pride is great up to the point you begin to throw out the baby with the bathwater. The rule of Satanism is: if it works for you, great. When it stops working for you, when you've painted yourself into a corner and the only way out is to say, I'm sorry, I made a mistake, I wish we could compromise somehow, then do it.

9. Lack of Aesthetics—This is the physical application of the Balance Factor. Aesthetics is important in Lesser Magic and should be cultivated. It is obvious that no one can collect any money off classical standards of beauty and form most of the time so they are discouraged in a consumer society, but an eye for beauty, for balance, is an essential Satanic tool and must be applied for greatest magical effectiveness. It's not what's supposed to be pleasing—it's what is. Aesthetics is a personal thing, reflective of one's own nature, but there are universally pleasing and harmonious configurations that should not be denied.

The investigator and priest should look for signs of occult involvement. Books, jewelry, artwork, ouija boards, crystal wands, statues, idols, symbols, etc. should all be watched for and if found taken from the premises and burned elsewhere by the priest himself. This should never be done on the same property as the client's residence. The purpose of this book is not to explore every cult or aspect of the occult. The investigator and priest is encouraged to engage in an independent study of the subject matter.

Notes:
1. Study the warnings of God to Israel regarding Satan and the occult: Deuteronomy 18:10- 12; Leviticus 17:7; 19:31; 20:16.
2. Study more about sacrifices made to devils: Deuteronomy 32:17; II Chronicles 11:15;Psalms 106:37.
3. The following are common characteristics of cults:
• Dictatorial Leadership: Cults cluster around domineering, charismatic personalities who have absolute authority and are accountable to no one.
• Exclusive: Cults adopt the attitude that they are the only group with divine truth. They exclude from fellowship others who disagree with them.
• Legalistic: Cults usually have strict rules of belief and behavior which have no Scriptural basis.
• Defensive: Cult members are usually led to believe that society, organized religion, and government are against them. This causes a reactionary attitude towards religion, government, and society.
• Oppressive: Cult members are usually manipulated and oppressed by the leadership.
• Secretive: Many things about the cult are kept secret from "outsiders".
• Higher Revelation: Cults often claim "higher revelation" from God. They will always have a source of authority beyond the Scriptures. It may be the writings or revelation of the founder or another person. In some cases it may be the founder's peculiar interpretation of the Bible. Their doctrines will not currently represent Biblical teachings.
• Anti-church: Cults vigorously oppose organized churches and their clergy.
• Anti-family: Cults are sometimes anti-family, which

means they want their members to break ties with family who are not members. They try to break biological family ties in order to retain their disciples.

4. There are so many cults world-wide that it is impossible to identify them all, but because of the increasing growth of what is called the "new age movement" major publishing houses in the United States now have "new age departments" because there is such a demand for their materials. The New Age movement has its roots in the ancient occultism. It has historical ties to Sumerian, Indian, Egyptian, Chaldean, Babylonian, and Persian religious practices. The "new age" is a fresh title, but the occult involved in it is nothing new. Jesus is considered just one of many "gods" or revealers of "truth" along with Buddha, Mohammed, Confucius, Zoroaster, Krishna, and many others. The deity of Jesus is denied. While the Church teaches man was separated from God by sin, the new age movement believes man is born inherently good. They believe he is separated from God only in his consciousness and is the victim of a false sense of separate identity that blinds him to his essential unity with God. Because of this, the new age movement advocates various methods of altering the consciousness such as yoga, meditation, chanting, ecstatic dancing, drugs, etc. They consider these a means to salvation. Because of these practices and involvement with witchcraft, sorcery, mediums, etc., new age practices open the door to demonic influences. Because they believe there is no evil, therefore there is no crime and no victim. Death is considered an illusion and because they believe a person is continually reincarnated, there are no victims of murder or abortion. The new age

methods of spreading propaganda include infiltration (even of the true Church) and unification through world-wide networking. New age members speak of a coming "purging" which will cleanse the world of all those "lesser evolved souls" who do not see themselves as gods. They are working towards the centralizing of power on a global level, an ungodly unity with man as the sole authority. The new age movement may be one of several forces through which Satan will culminate his plans for global unification. It could very possibly could be the platform upon which the antichrist will rise to world-wide domination.

5. Study II Peter chapter 2 and the book of Jude. List characteristics that will help you detect Satan's messengers in the church.

CHAPTER FIVE
FIGHTING THE DEMONIC

How God anointed Jesus of Nazareth with the Holy Ghost and with power: who went about doing good, and healing all that were oppressed of the Devil; for God was with Him. -Acts 10:38

The life of Christ clearly demonstrated that demonic entities are a reality. What Christ taught about demons and how He dealt with them yields valuable information about the strategies of Satan. Christ taught that Satan is the ruler of demons. He taught of the reality and power of demons. He said that the casting out of demonic entities was one of the signs that the Kingdom of God had come. A large portion of the ministry of Christ involved dealing with demons. It is the example of Christ and the authority of His name bestowed on those in Apostolic Succession that provides the legitimate basis for dealing with the demonic. Christ ministered to "all" who came with demonic afflictions. The Apostle Peter said of Christ:

... God anointed Jesus of Nazareth with the Holy Ghost and with power: who went about doing good, and healing all that were oppressed of the devil.
-Acts 10:38

Demons are used by Satan to oppose God, His plan and purposes, and His Church. They also war against Christians to keep them from the truth of the Gospel and from participation in the Church Militant. Demons control specific physical localities (principalities) such as the prince of Persia mentioned in Daniel 10:12-13.Demons also work through people to accomplish Satanic objectives in the world. Opposition to God's will is Satan's main objective. The word "Satan" means "adversary." Satan is primarily God's adversary (Job 1:6; Matthew 13:39). He is secondarily, humanity's adversary (Zechariah 3:1; I Peter 5:8). As you have already learned, demons have different natures. Remember that one demon identified himself in I Kings 22:23 as a "lying spirit." A "deaf and dumb" spirit is identified in Mark 9:25. Demons of various natures operate as spirits of infirmity, seducing spirits, and unclean spirits. Satan uses them to afflict humanity in body and spirit.

Demons of Infirmity- These are demonic entities that can afflict the bodies of Christians as well as unbelievers. Read Luke 13:10- 17. This woman was afflicted with a spirit of infirmity. She was present in the Sabbath services and Christ called her "a daughter of Abraham." Yet her body had been afflicted by Satan for eighteen years. For other examples of demonic powers afflicting the body see Matthew 12:22; 17:15-18; Acts 10:38; II Corinthians 12:7.

Seductive Demons- These spirits afflict the spirit of man, seducing him to believe doctrinal lies and be condemned to eternal punishment. They are the spirits of false doctrine, cults, false Christs, and false teachers:

Now the Spirit speaketh expressly, that in the latter times some shall depart from the faith, giving heed to

seducing spirits, and doctrines of devils.
-I Timothy 4:1

**These seducing spirits are deceptive. They actually
work miracles which lead some to believe they are of
God: For they are the spirits of devils, working
miracles, which go forth unto the kings of the earth
and of the whole world, to gather them to the battle
of that great day of God Almighty. -Revelation 16:14**

Seducing spirits include the "spirit of divination"
mentioned in Acts:

**And it came to pass, as we went to prayer, a certain
damsel possessed with a spirit of divination met us,
which brought her masters much gain by
soothsaying. -Acts 16:16**

Such spirits of divination or "familiar spirits" operate in
psychics, channelers, sensitives, shamans and those who
advocate spirit guides. Through pagan, New Age and
even more blatantly Satanic methods the spirits of
divination foretell the future or discover knowledge
which is naturally unknown. Warnings against familiar
spirits are given in Leviticus 19:31; 20:6; Deuteronomy
5:9; 18:10; Leviticus 20:27; and I Samuel 28:3.
Seducing spirits sear the conscience, seduce, entice,
tempt, allure, interest, fascinate, excite, arouse, attract,
and deceive. Seducing spirits are active in causing
"spiritual wickedness in high places." They are present
in every cult and wherever false teaching is promoted.
Seducing spirits entice men and women to worship idols
and even Satan himself.

Unclean Demons- These demonic entities afflict the nature of man. They are responsible for immoral acts, unclean thoughts, temptations and other strategies of Satan used to bind men and women. When Satan controls individuals with unclean spirits, he can also operate in homes, churches, and entire nations as these groups are composed of individuals. This is how Satan works in the various levels of structure in society. For examples of unclean spirits see Matthew 10:1; 12:43; and Mark 1:23-26. The priest should be prepared for all manner of sexually explicit language, talk, and even enticements when dealing with such demons. Intercessors and investigators are cautioned NOT to give heed to the things these and other demons say and/or do. The goal is to shock, stun, cause doubt, and ultimately entice the mind to ponder things of an immoral nature greatly reducing the effectiveness of the exorcism process.

OPPRESSION, OBSESSION, POSSESSION

Demonic entities can oppress people. To oppress means to bear down, come against, or bind from the outside. This oppression is accomplished by demons in various ways. They cause depression, create negative circumstances, and insert wrong thoughts into the mind such as thoughts of suicide, immorality, unbelief, fear, etc. Demons create Satanic circumstances and situations which tempt men to sin:

How God anointed Jesus of Nazareth with the Holy Ghost and with power: who went about doing good, and healing all that were OPPRESSED of the Devil; for God was with Him. -Acts 10:38

Demons can also possess the human body. Demon possession is a condition in which one or more demons inhabit the body of a human being and take complete control of their victim at will. "Possession" does not mean a person is not responsible for his or her own personal sin. The responsibility rests with the factors that led to his/her condition. Possession can happen willingly. A person may desire to be taken over by demonic entities in order to conduct seances, pronounce curses, become a witch, or secure some other supernatural power. Possession can also occur unwilling. An individual does not ask to be possessed, but through sinful thoughts, actions, or contact with the occult possession results. Demonic powers operating in parents and the sins of the parents can affect the next generation. (See Exodus 20:5; 34:7; and Deuteronomy 5:9.) This accounts for demon possession or oppression of children such as recorded in Mark 7:24-30 and 9:17-21.There is also such a thing as demon obsession. This is a condition where one becomes obsessed by an interest in or preoccupation with demons. It is an unusual interest in the occult, demons, and Satan which controls interests and pursuits in a dictating manner. Such obsession with demon powers can lead to possession.

CAN DEMONS ATTACK CHRISTIANS?
They can, but it is made much more difficult because the Holy Spirit cannot inhabit the same temple as a demonic entity:

What? Know ye not that your body is the temple of the Holy Ghost which is in you, which ye have of

**God, and ye are not your own? For ye are bought
with a price: Therefore glorify God in your body,
and in your spirit, which are God's.
-I Corinthians 6:19-20**

When you become a Christian, are baptized and confirmed (filled with the Holy Spirit), you cannot belong to Satan and be filled with his spirits at the same time. The Holy Spirit will not abide in the same "temple" with Satan. But this does not mean Christians cannot be affected by demonic entities. It is these powers against which we wrestle. Satan uses demonic powers to attack believers from the outside through oppression, the symptoms of which were previously discussed. But he cannot possess the dedicated Christian, except with divine permission (these cases are very rare). To "possess" indicates internal occupation. To "oppress" or bind indicates control or severe influence from the outside. The activities of Christians can be demonically manipulated if they allow demonic entities to oppress them. Such oppression permits Satan to use the client for evil purposes. This is what happened when Peter, a disciple of Jesus, was used of Satan to try to divert Jesus from suffering for the sins of all mankind. When Jesus described the suffering He was to go through, Peter said:

**...Be it far from thee, Lord: this shall not be unto
thee. -Matthew 16:22**

Jesus said to Peter:

**...Get thee behind me, Satan: thou art an offence
unto me: for thou savourest not the things that be of**

God, but those that be of men. -Matthew 16:23

Jesus did not mean Peter was actually Satan. He recognized that at that moment Peter had allowed Satan to operate through him. He was not demon possessed, but he was allowing Satanic spirits to influence him.

Believers, by their own actions, give place or make room for Satan to use them. -Ephesians 4:27

When a person is baptized and confirmed in the Holy Orthodox Faith, his name is written in a special book in Heaven called the book of life. Only those whose names are in this book will be residents of Heaven for eternity.

And whosoever was not found written in the book of life was cast into thelake of fire. -Revelation 20:15

It is possible to have your name written in the book of life, but later blotted out because of turning back to sinful living:

He that overcometh, the same shall be clothed in white raiment; and I will not blot out his name out of the book of life, but I will confess his name before my Father, and before His angels. -Revelation 3:5

If a Christian continues in known, unconfessed sin, there is a point at which he can cease to be a Christian. The Apostle Paul expressed his own concern that he not be "cast away" after preaching to others:

But I keep under my body, and bring it into subjection: lest that by any means, when I have preached to others, I myself should be a castaway.
-I Corinthians 9:27

Paul realized that sin, especially continued unconfessed sins of the flesh, could result in the loss of his own soul even though he had preached to others. By continuing to live in sin the client will eventually end up in a condition of serious mortal sin which after a prolonged period of time removes them from participation in the mystical Body of Christ. This means they are no longer a true follower of Jesus Christ. When this state occurs, the client has opened his or herself up to greater attacks of the Adversary, including the possibility of demonic possession. This is why it is important when you sin to immediately confess all sin to a priest and turn from unrighteousness:

If we confess our sins, He is faithful and just to forgive us our sins, and to cleanse us from all unrighteousness. If we say that we have not sinned, we make Him a liar, and His Word is not in us.
- I John 1:9-10

In all cases the priest should strongly encourage nonbelievers to embrace the faith, be baptized and confirmed, and make a good confession. If the family are Christian they are encouraged to embrace the Ancient Holy Orthodox Catholic Faith, make a good confession individually, and then seek the solace of pastoral counseling which may or may not include exorcism of property or persons, depending on the need.

DEMONIC CONTROL
Demons gain control in several ways:

1. **Through generations-** Demons may oppress or possess a person or family because of previous possession or oppression of the parents. This accounts for demonic influence over children (Exodus 20:5; 34:7; Deuteronomy 5:9).
2. **Through the mind-** If Satan can control the clients thoughts, he will eventually control their actions. Lack of mental control eventually results in lack of use of the will. This leads to sinful actions. Continuing in sinful thoughts and actions can lead from oppression to possession and finally to a reprobate mind such as is described in Romans chapter one. This is a mind totally controlled by evil thoughts. Demons also gain access through mind-altering drugs which reduce the ability to resist demons and grant increasing access. "hypnosis" or "mind control" techniques also provides an entrance point.
3. **Through sinful actions-** Sinful thoughts are soon fulfilled by sinful actions. For example, the thought of adultery is fulfilled in the actual act of adultery. Sin is rebellion, and rebellious thoughts and actions provides an entry point for demonic activity. When a Christian continues in sinful thoughts or actions they "give place" to the demonic (Ephesians 4:27). Sins of involvement with the occult, including objects, literature, seances, etc., are actions which are especially dangerous and attract demonic entities. A

Christian who lives in sin is open not only to oppression of demonic entities, but also possession. As you have learned, there is no neutral ground in spiritual warfare. You are either on the side of good or evil. You belong either to God or Satan.

4. **Through desire-** Some people desire and request of Satan to be under the control of demons powers. They do this for purposes of having supernatural power or performing supernatural acts. Those with "spirit guides" or "psychic ability" should NEVER be used in an investigation nor consulted for any reason whatsoever.

5. **Through an empty "house"-** Demons consider the body of the person they inhabit as their house (Matthew 12:44). When a person who has been delivered from demonic possession does not fill his spiritual house with the Holy Spirit, reentry may occur.

6. **Through permission-** Sometimes God grants permission for activities of demonic entities to accomplish special purposes. This can be allowed as a trial of Christians as in the case of Job. It can also be judgment for sin as in the case of King Saul.

WHO IS TO ACT AS EXORCIST?

Dealing with demonic entities is not something to be engaged in by paranormal investigators, ghost hunters or demonologists. Christ conveyed this authority only to the Apostles and their successors (bishops and priests in Apostolic Succession):

And these signs shall follow them that believe: In my name shall they cast out devils... -Mark 16:17

And when He had called unto Him His twelve disciples, He gave them power against unclean spirits, to cast them out, and to heal all manner of sickness and all manner of disease. -Matthew 10:1

And He called unto Him the twelve, and began to send them forth by two and two; and gave them power over unclean spirits. -Mark 6:7

And these signs shall follow them that believe: In my name shall they cast out devils... -Mark 16:17

Heal the sick, cleanse the lepers, raise the dead, cast out devils: freely ye have received, freely give. -Matthew 10:8

However, even priests should not rush into exorcism without proper preparation, as the sons of Sceva discovered (Acts 19). It is also important that priests in this area of ministry do not become overly demon conscious. We are not called to be "demon hunters". We are called to be priests of the Most High, to offer the unbloody sacrifice of the Holy Mass, and to tend His flock. Those who are too fascinated with this area of ministry, or who seem to delight in its discussion are not suitable exorcists and should not be mentored.

DETECTING DEMONIC PRESENCE

To overcome demonic powers it is important to be able to recognize their presence and tactics. The Holy Spirit has provided a special spiritual gift for this purpose. This gift is called "discerning of spirits" (I Corinthians 12:10). To discern means "to discover, evaluate, and make a distinction between." The gift of discerning of spirits enables a priest to discern the spirits operating in others. It permits him to discover, evaluate, and identify evil spirits. The gift of discerning of spirits is very important when dealing with preternatural investigation. It enables you to discern whether or not a person has a demonic entity operating through or against him. It prevents deception by recognizing when other more plausible answers are available. The well trained exorcist/priest is also able to recognize the evil tactics and motives of demonic entities. Here are some symptoms of demonic activity:

Demonic obsession- Recognized by an uncontrollable and unusual preoccupation with demons, Satan, or the occult. Such a person may dabble in occult practices, constantly credit everything to Satan or demons, or be preoccupied with the study of demons and Satan.

Demonic oppression- Recognized by the following signs:
1. A physical binding: The "daughter of Abraham" who Jesus relieved of a spirit of infirmity was bound physically. See Luke 13:10-17. Chronic sickness may be demonic oppression. All illness is not caused by demonic powers. Some illness is caused by a violation of natural laws, such as not eating properly or drinking bad water. Some illness is also chastisement.

2. A mental oppression- Disturbances in the mind or

thought life such as mental torment, confusion, doubt, loss of memory, missing time, etc. Restlessness, inability to reason or listen to others, abnormal talkativeness or reserve may be exhibited. All mental problems are not caused by Satan. Discouragement, depression, and disorientation can be caused by allergies to certain foods or a wrong chemical imbalance in the brain. Caution should be taken not to class illness or mental problems as being caused by demonic entities. Sometimes a simple change in diet or lifestyle will eliminate a problem if it is caused by physical causes. Always defer to medical and psychological professionals.

3. Emotional problems: Disturbances in the emotions which persist or recur, including resentment, hatred, anger, fear, rejection, self-pity, jealousy, depression, worry, insecurity, inferiority, etc.

4. Spiritual problems: Extreme difficulties in overcoming sin, including sinful habits. Rejection of spiritual solutions to problems. Any type of doctrinal error or deception, including bondage to objects and literature of the cults.

5. Circumstances: Demons can create difficult circumstances which are oppressive. Such circumstances usually involve confusion and can immediately be identified as demonic because God is not the author of confusion (I Corinthians 14:33; James 3:16).

Demonic possession- Recognized by the following

signs:

1. Indwelling of an unclean spirit: This is demonstrated by a basic moral uncleanness and filthiness. It might include the desire to go without clothing. For examples see Mark 5:2 and Luke 8:27.

2. Unusual physical strength: A person shows strength beyond normal capabilities. For examples see Mark 5:3 and Luke 8:29.

3. Fits of rage: These fits may be accompanied by foaming at the mouth. See Mark 9:14-29 and Luke 8:26-39.

4. Resistance to spiritual things: In the accounts in Mark 6:7 and 1:21-28, the demons knew Jesus immediately and asked Him to leave them alone. Fear of the name of Jesus, the saints, holy objects, holy places, prayer, and the Word of God and blasphemy of that which is spiritual are all symptoms of demon possession. Excessive blasphemy may be noted or contorted physical features and abrupt behavior changes when spiritual things are mentioned.

5. Changes in personality and/or voice: A person who is normally shy may become aggressive or violent. Actions as well as appearance may be affected. Moral character and intelligence may change. Voice may be altered. See Mark 5:9.

6. Accompanying physical afflictions: In cases of demon possession, these appear most commonly to be afflictions of the mental and nervous system. (See Matthew 9:33; 12:22; Mark 5:4-5). They can also include a general "pining" or wasting away physically. (See Mark 9:14-29).

7. Self-inflicted physical injury: In Matthew 17:14-21 there is the story of a man's son who would cast himself

in the fire. In Luke 8:26-39 this demon possessed man cut himself with stones to inflict physical injury.

8. Terrible anguish: Luke 8:28 relates that this man went about crying because of the terrible inner torments caused by his possession.

9. Incapacity for normal living: This man could not live in society but lived in the tombs of the cemetery. See Luke 8:27.

10. Through unscriptural methods, the ability to foretell the future or discover that which is unknown: The woman in Acts 16:16 is said to be "possessed" by a spirit of divination.

11. Speaking in a language unknown to the client, especially a dead language such as Latin. Sometimes languages such as Aramaic, Urdu, Sanskrit, etc. are encountered.

The following also may indicate demonic oppression or obsession:

1. Obsessive immorality such as involvement with extreme forms of pornography, adultery, fornication, masturbation, homosexuality, and other sex sins.
2. Strong compulsions toward eating disorders, suicide, self-mutilation, maiming, and murder.
3. Addiction to drugs or alcohol.
4. Trances, visions, and meditation which are not focused on or from the one true God.
5. Bondage to emotions such as fear, anxiety, depression, hatred, rage, jealousy, backbiting, envy, pride, bitterness, negativism, and criticism

SIMPLE PRIESTLY PREPARATION

• Make a good and complete confession.

• Fast at least three days before the exorcism.

• Offer the Holy Sacrifice of the Mass, pray the Breviary, and attend devotions.
• Discuss the experiences with your assistant after each session.
Disregard all the things the demonic entity will say, reveal, and entice you with, as well as manifest experiences you may see. Accept that the New Testament means exactly what it says. Accept it as true and act accordingly. You are the representative of Christ (II Corinthians 5:20).

INTERCESSOR PREPARATION
Whenever possible, a team of intercessors should be used when binding or casting out demons. Jesus sent out His disciples in pairs for this ministry:

And He called unto Him the twelve, and began to send them forth by two and two: and gave them power over unclean spirits. -Mark 6:7

This does not mean you cannot be effective alone, but there is strength in unity of prayer. Since strength comes from unity, those who are joining you in the exorcism should be similarly prepared with prayer and fasting. In cases of oppression and obsession, prepare the client. They need to have their faith built. (This may not be possible in the case of possession). Proper spiritual instruction must be given. Sometimes, God delivers without such instruction. But in exorcism ministry you want to properly use every channel prescribed by the Church to see the work done. Faith is one channel for God's delivering power and it comes by hearing God's Word, so instruction is important. Christ combined preaching and teaching with healing and deliverance and He instructed His followers to do so also.

THE PLACE OF EXORCISM
The ritual of exorcism is more properly performed in a Church, monastery, convent or rectory. Many have the misguided notion that this occurs in the bedroom of the victim only. As a priest you must understand that exorcism is a valid ministry of the Church. However, it is not necessary or even practical to do so in every case. Christ cast out the demons whenever and wherever he found them.

THE TIME OF EXORCISM
When you are ready to begin an exorcism session the following are basic guidelines of how best to proceed.

1. **Begin with a hymn-** We enter the presence of Christ the King through worship and praise. Singing hymns or Gregorian chants establish an environment of holiness.
2. **Pray first-** Ask for wisdom and discernment before you begin the ritual.
3. **Determine whether to continue with the ritual-** Determine whether or not to repeat the ritual during a session or wait until another date. In most cases, you will pray the ritual, but in some, do not be surprised if the Lord directs you not to pray or to delay prayer. Jesus delayed healing in the case of the Syrophonecian woman's daughter and Lazarus. He did not do many works at all in Nazareth because of unbelief. The Lord may also direct you to delay until further instruction is

given, i.e., they may need to deal with a sin problem, need more instruction, a curse or occult object is revealed, etc.

4. **Pray the ritual exactly as it is worded-**Stick to the text exactly. Deviation causes weakness in the process and disturbs the focus of the ritual itself.Do not spend time talking with the demon, should it manifest itself through spoken words outside what is required by the ritual. Jesus rebuked demons and told them to be quiet (Luke 4:34-35). Remember that any conversation with demons is dangerous because there are lying spirits. When forced to speak to the demon use the following as preperatory commands:

"In the name of Jesus Christ and on the basis of the authority of His power, His Word, His blood, and the Holy Spirit..."
...This establishes the power base for exorcism...

"...I bind you...."
...Christ taught to bind the demonic first before attempting to cast him out...

"...and I command you..."
...Exorcism is a prayer of priestly authority, not of entreaty. You can speak quietly, but you must take authority over the forces of evil in the name of Christ. Look directly into the eyes of the person as you speak.

"...the spirit of_____" or "...you foul spirit of Satan..."
...if the spirit has been identified either through spiritual

or natural discernment, then name it specifically; otherwise, generally.

"...to depart...."
...this is the casting out process...

"...without harming_____(name of person being exorcized), or anyone in this house, and without creating noise or disturbance"
...Sometimes the demon will try to harm the person or create disturbance.

"I forbid you to reenter this person..."
...Remember that Christ used this command...

SIGNS OF RELEASE

In cases of demonic possession, sometimes the demons come out with a struggle, such as crying out or throwing the person on the floor. When demons have departed (whether in possession or oppression), there will be a sense of release, joy, like the lifting of a weight. The victim will be able to receive holy objects, bless themselves with holy water, receive blessings, pray, etc.

ONGOING COUNSELING

After exorcism, those who have been possessed by demons should receive ongoing pastoral counseling and integration into the community life of the Church. When a demon is cast out, he will seek another body through which to operate. Christ taught that the departure of evil spirits leaves an empty place. There is danger of a demon returning to his former victim accompanied by worse spirits:

When the unclean spirit is gone out of a man, he walketh through dry places, seeking rest; and finding none, he saith, I will return unto my house whence I came out. And when he cometh he findeth it swept and garnished. Then goeth he, and taketh to him seven other spirits more wicked than himself; and they enter in, and dwell there; and the last state of that man is worse than the first. -Luke 11:24-26

When a demon is cast out it is restless and discontent outside of a human body. It is only by indwelling and controlling a human life that a demon is able to fulfill Satan's evil purposes. This is why casting the demon out is not enough. Follow up counseling and ministry is necessary. The person should be immersed in the Word of God and prayer and become part of the Church, receiving the Sacraments as often as absolutely possible.

SACERDOTAL
ADDENDUM

When you minister to a person experiencing demonic activity, you will almost always encounter a variety of elements that may be keys in keeping the person in spiritual turmoil. There are often unresolved hurts, spiritual issues, etc. that need to be addressed. Balanced pastoral counseling involves much more than simply praying the ritual of exorcism.

Investigation

The first step in preternatural counseling is investigation of all claims. What we do in this process is determine whether the person is really in need of exorcism on either a personal or property level, or if there are other plausible reasons for the perceived phenomenon. This is a vital step that saves a lot of time and helps ensure that the clients physical, emotional, psychological, and spiritual needs are met. If you enter into a case with the preconceived notion that the person is in need of exorcism you may add very dangerous imagery to potential psychological issues which may be the real cause. You also leave yourself open to litigation and can waste precious time and resources. Before a person is permitted to even undergo exorcism, they must meet the following requirements:

1. They must be a Christian- If they are not, then it is extremely dfficult to exorcize a demonic entity. How can there be an effective exorcism without the confession forgiveness of sins, or without the baptism and confirmation of Christ's Church? It is vital that the person be baptized, confirmed, and make a confession before you can effectively pray the ritual of exorcism on their behalf. Exorcism is geared towards the Church Militant (Christians faithful to the historic faith).

2. They must be willing to give up all areas of sin- Example: If a client enjoys pornography and is unwilling to give it up, then it will be nearly impossible to cast out a demon that may be oppressing them with obssesive thoughts and diabolic temptation regarding sexual perversions without it coming right back. Please understand that it is possible to enjoy pornography or feel attracted to it, and yet be willing to let go of it at the same time. They must be willing to destroy these strongholds in order to receive and maintain their freedom the demonic. Furthermore, and this is very important; they must be willing to communicate about their past openly with you as their priest. It is important that you, as a priest, are aware of the areas of sin in their life, and the underlying roots of those sins. If they choose to hide something from you, it may very well keep you from being able to effectively exorcize the demonic entity.

3. They must be willing to convert to the historic Catholic faith and enter the life of the Church Militant- This often involves taking catechism lessons, being baptized, confirmed, making confession, receiving the Sacraments, reading the writings of the Saints, and daily Sacred Scripture reading and prayer. Doing this is vital to the tearing down of strongholds. They must be serious enough about their relationship with Christ, that they take His Church seriously. Counseling individuals who are not established in the Ancient Holy Orthodox Christian Faith can be more time consuming and burdensome. It is much easier to counsel an individual who is strongly connected to the Church. However, in some cases, having this luxury is not possible, as by the time many desperate individuals come to us, there is little time to do everything we might like.

QUESTIONNAIRE
The interview process and questionnaire are meant to be used by knowledgeable investigators and priests, because the reasons for each of these questions is not explained in this questionnaire. A knowledgeable investigator or priest should know the reasons behind each of these questions. This insight is gained through proper mentorship to an experienced investigator or priest.

Part I
1. When did this start?
2. Was there any unusual things that took place (or you did) when this bondage started?
3. If this started when you were a child: Do you have ancestors who have suffered from a similar kind of experience?
4. What kind of experiences are you facing? (Fears, depression, voices in your mind, mental illness, physical illness, mental torment, spiritual torment, etc.. Please be as detailed as possible.)
5. What are all the things that have impacted your life?

(Parent's death, trauma, a certain situation that changed your life, anything that 'changed' you.)

Part II

1. Do you have ancestors who have struggled with similar problems or mental illness?
2. Did your bondage start as a child and appear to have no reason to be there?
3. Do you have siblings who suffer from similar problems or oppression?

Part III

1. Have you been involved with extramarital sex? Are you attracted to an ex-lover? Is he or she a good/godly influence for you?
2. Have you been divorced?
3. Do you feel an unusual attraction to a past boyfriend, girlfriend or lover (who is obviously not right for you)?
4. Do you let anybody dominate, control, or make your choices you?
5. Have you ever formed a blood covenant with another person? (Blood brothers, etc.)
6. Have you ever made vows or agreements with somebody in effort to strengthen the relationship or commit yourself to each other?
7. Do you see any ungodly relationships in your past where gifts were exchanged? (Are you holding onto something that was given to you from somebody you had an adultery with, etc.)
8. Have you ever had ungodly relations with an animal?
9. Do you have any pictures in your possession of

somebody whom you may have an ungodly soul tie with? (A picture of you with somebody you had an adultery with, etc.)

Part IV

1. What do you think of your parents?
2. How would you explain your childhood?
3. Were you close to your parents while growing up? If not, why?
4. How would you explain your relationship with your parents? Was it good, bad or very cold?
5. Did you feel rejection from your parents?
6. Were either of your parents overly passive or controlling?
7. Have either of your parents been divorced? Remarried? Are your parents divorced?
8. How would you describe your relationship with your siblings growing up?

Part V

1. Were your parents married when you were conceived? Were you the right gender? Did your parents not want you, or want you to be different (gender, etc.) in any way? If so, explain.
2. Did you feel rejected as a child? As an adult? If so, by whom? Explain.
3. Did you face abuse? What kind (emotional, physical, sexual, etc.) and by whom?
4. Have you faced rejection from your peers, classmates, friends or those around you?
5. Have you ever been put down, belittled, or made fun of? If so, by whom? Explain.

6. If you have faced rejection or abuse, how did you respond? Do you feel you are still paying a price for it? If so, how?

7. How do you respond to rejection right now?

8. Do you reject yourself ? If so, why and in what ways?

Part VI

1. Is there anybody you feel edgy around? (Don't like them, feel anything in your heart against them, etc.)

2. Do you have anything against anybody? In other words, is there anybody that you have a hard time demonstrating the love of Christ to?

3. Has anybody wronged you that you haven't forgiven from your heart (thoughts, feelings, emotions, etc.)?

4. How do your view your siblings, parents, coworkers, etc.? Do you have any hard feelings against them?

5. Do you make a habit of blaming yourself for everything? Do you obsess over your mistakes and feel unusually guilty for them?

6. Do you deeply regret things that you've done in your past? Could you kick yourself over something you've done in your past? If so, explain.

Part VII

1. Are you a very positive or negative person?

2. Do you feel confident? If so, why?

3. Do you have a low self esteem? If so, why?

4. Are you domineering or controlling? If so, to whom, and in what ways? Why?

5. Are you an achiever? If so, in what ways?

6. Do you feel that you are always right and that if

everybody did everything your way, this world would be a better place to live?

7. How do you treat your children? Husband? Are you controlling, passive, etc.?

8. Do you like people to 'look at you' (as in receive attention)?

Part VIII

1. Do you strive to feel accepted? If so, how does this affect your lifestyle? By whom do you want to feel accepted?

2. Are you always stressed out? If so, why?

3. Do you feel hurt? If so, by whom/what and why?

4. Do you feel good about yourself? If not, why?

5. Do you feel depressed? If so, why? When did it start? Did your parents or grandparents struggle with depression? If so, then do you know when it started and why? Do you have siblings who are also struggling? Do you feel your depression is rational or irrational?

6. Do you struggle with fears? If so, what is it that you fear? (Fear of heights, dying, being hopeless, failure, never marrying, etc.)

7. Do you worry about things? What things do you worry about? Why?

8. Do you struggle with anger? Do you have a short temper?

9. Do you have any insecurities? If so, explain.

10. Do you feel any self-pity or feel sorry for yourself? Have you ever felt this? If so, why?

11. Do you find it easy to hate people? If so, over what kinds of things would a person have to do to make you hate them?

12. Do you have any irrational feelings? If so, what are they?

13. Do you feel like something is wrong with you?

14. Do you feel excessively guilty over anything? Is this a continual problem?

15. Are you very confused and forgetful? (Beyond the normal)

16. Are you aware of any emotional wounds that have affected you?

17. Have you ever been deeply embarrassed over something? What was it?

18. Have you been in or are currently experiencing very difficult (depressing) circumstances which may cause you to feel hopeless or depressed?

Part IX

1. How do you explain your relationship with God?

2. Do you feel you aren't good enough to meet His standards?

3. Do you see Him as a loving father, or a dictator?

4. Do you believe that it's only by the Blood of Jesus that your sins are forgiven? Or do you feel you need to earn your forgiveness in any way?

5. Do you feel God's love in your life?

6. Do you feel like your sins are forgiven? Or do you feel guilty?

7. Do you feel excessively guilty in everyday life?

8. Do you feel that doing good things, you earn God's love and acceptance?

9. Do you feel that God is angry or upset with you?

Part X

1. Have you ever spoken something negative about yourself that has came to pass?
2. Have your parents, or those in authority over you spoken a curse over you?
3. Have you ever made a vow out of anger? If so, what?
4. Have you ever wished to die? Have you ever said it?
5. If you have made any vows or oaths, what are they?

Part XI

1. Do you have many friends? What kind of people are they?
2. Do you have a hard time trying to meet new people or make friends?
3. Are you socially outgoing or shy? If so, why?
4. How would you define your relationship with your spouse?

Part XII

1. Have you ever had immoral sexual relations? What kind? (Fornication, adultery, sodomy, bestiality, with a child, etc.)
2. Have you struggled with lust, fantasy or unholy sexual thoughts? If so, what kind?
3. Have you been attracted to pornography?
4. Do you have homosexual thoughts and desires? If so, have you acted upon those feelings?
5. How do you feel about your sexuality? (Do you feel dirty about it, or do you feel it's a wonderful blessing that God's given you?)

6. Do you withhold sex from your spouse or are you fidgety? Do you enjoy a healthy relationship with your spouse sexually? How does he or she react?

7. Have you ever been raped or sexually abused?

8. Have you ever woke up and felt a sexual presence with you?

9. Do you struggle or have you struggled with masturbation?

10. Do you struggle or have you struggled with any other sexual related thoughts, desires, or bondages?

11. Is there anything sexually that you are ashamed of?

Part XIII

1. Do you have any addictions? If so, what kind? (Drugs, alcohol, smoking, eating, sex, TV, etc.) When did they start?

2. Did anybody else in your family (siblings, ancestors, etc.) have a struggle with any addictions? If so, what? Who?

3. Have you ever had, or currently have any sort of obsession over anything? If so, what?

Part XIV

1. Have you ever been involved with any false religions? If so, why, when and how long? How do you feel about those beliefs now?

2. Have you ever been involved in any secret societies such as Freemasonry? If so, how deep were you involved?

Part XV

1. Have you ever shown interest in the occult? If so, in what ways? (Read up on it, dabbled in it, etc.)
2. Do you still feel drawn or attracted to the occult?
3. Have you had any interest in horror or thriller style movies or novels? Are you still attracted to these things?
4. Have you ever made a vow with the devil? If so, what?
5. Married Satan?
6. Worshipped a demon or Satan?
7. Have you ever put a curse or spell on somebody?
8. Are you aware of any curses or spells placed on you? If so, what? Who did it?
9. Dabbled with an Ouija board? If so, why?
10. Ever been a member of a coven? Explain.
11. Communicated with the dead? Explain.
12. Told somebody's fortune or went to see a psychic? Explain.
13. Ever read your horoscope?
14. Watched or been involved in a séance? Explain.
15. Been involved in New Age teachings? Explain.
16. Been initiated in a false religion? If so, what were you initiated into? When?
17. Have you ever had a spirit guide?
18. Have you ever been involved with meditation, yoga, reiki, or related activities?
19. Were you or anybody in your family superstitious? If so, who?
20. Ever been involved in astral travel? (Out of body)
21. If you have made any vows or oaths, what are they? Were there any sacrifices or rituals that was accompanied with them?

22. Have you ever made a blood pact before? If so, with whom (including persons, demons and Satan) and for what purpose?

23. Have you ever partaken in automatic writing, automatic drawing or automatic painting?

25. Any other involvement in the occult? Explain.

Part XVI

1. Are there any un-confessed sins? (Usually something you've done, that you know is wrong, but won't admit to it. An abortion, stealing, etc. are some examples.)

2. Is there anything you've been hiding inside that you haven't confessed?

3. Do you feel excessively guilty over some thing(s) you've done in the past? If so, what?

Part XVII

1. Do you have any idols, occult objects, or anything that could hold evil spiritual value in your home? If so, what? Any objects that hold evil spiritual value must be destroyed.

2. Do you have any gifts saved from sinful relationships? If so, explain. For example, if a man gives a woman a personal gift during an adultery, that needs to be sold or destroyed.

Part XVIII

1. Have you ever been exposed to extreme abuse or a traumatic experience? Did it have a drastic effect on your emotional or mental system? If so, what happen?

How did it affect you?

2. Have you ever been diagnosed with Dissociative Identity Disorder (DID)?

3. Are you aware of any alters (other personalities) that you may have? (If so, tell me about them)

4. Do you have a memory gap where you cannot remember a certain time of your life?

5. Do you have false memories of things that really didn't take place?

6. Have you ever been in a car accident or other traumatic situation? Have you ever witnessed a tragedy in real life?

7. Do you feel you were abducted by "aliens"? Explain.

Part XIX

1. Do you struggle with any habitual sins? If so, what? Do you want to break those bad habits?

2. Do you struggle with any weaknesses such as lust, anger, hate, etc.? If so, what? Do you know where they came from or how they got started?

Part XX

1. Have you ever said something along the lines of, "I will never have children"?

2. Have you ever had an abortion or attempted one?

3. Have you ever had incest or ungodly sexual relations with somebody related to you? (See Leviticus 20:19-21, as this can cause a curse to land upon you which needs to be broken)

Part XXI

1. Have you ever tried drugs? If so, how much, and how did it affect you? Why did you try drugs?
2. Have you ever thought about or attempted suicide?
3. Do you have any physical or mental disabilities, diseases or illnesses? Explain.
4. Do you want, and are willing to be delivered? Are you willing to make some lifestyle changes in order to be delivered?
5. Do you experience unusual confusion settle upon you as you try to pray, attend Mass, and read the Bible?
6. What kind of music do you like? (Please list all styles of music you currently enjoy, and give examples in each category you list, such as some names of artists and songs)
7. Have you previously enjoyed hard rock, metal, acid, alternative, rap, new age, or any other kind of worldly music? (Please provide some examples of artists and songs from each genre (type/style) of music you list)
8. Have you had any nightmares or weird experiences at night while supposedly sleeping?
9. Have you ever been in a trance or had an out of body experience?
10. Have you ever noticed time slipped right out from under you? For example, you look at your watch and it's 7:00pm, then you look again what seemed like 15 minutes later and it's 2:00am. This is a sign of a trance.
11. Have you ever touched or kissed a dead body? If so, explain whom and why and what happened afterwards.
12. Do you feel that you somehow have to earn your forgiveness? Do you 'wonder' if your sins are truly forgiven -- all of them?

13. Do you have any physical infirmities, sickness or diseases? If so, please list them.
14. Are you on any medications? If so, please explain.
15. Have you ever had any other kind of weird encounter with the spiritual realm?

What are some of the signs of a possessed house?

There are many signs we can look for in a possessed home or building. Some of the things a person can look for are doors slamming when nobody is there, strange noises, reputation for calamities (people being pushed down stairs, finances always being drained, etc.), the air seems heavy (making it harder to breathe), animals acting fearful or weird (dogs barking like mad for no reason), and so forth. Often somebody with spiritual discernment will often pick up on a spiritual presence that doesn't feel right. It's not uncommon to visit a home and pick up on demonic presence before even finding out that there was demonic activity that's taken place there. I've picked up on something demonic before even entering a home before... just standing on the property is enough to sense out an unclean presence.

How do homes and land become demonically inhabited?

Sins of the inhabitants: One of the ways which a place can become defiled is through the deeds of its inhabitants. If things such as seances, voodoo, adultery, or incest have been practiced in a home, then demonic spirits may inhabit there. Sacred Scripture tells us that the deeds of its inhabitants can defile even the land on which it is practiced:

Leviticus 18:24-25,27, "Defile not ye yourselves in any of these things: for in all these the nations are defiled which I cast out before you: And the land is defiled: therefore I do visit the iniquity thereof upon it, and the land itself vomiteth out her inhabitants... (For all these abominations have the men of the land done, which [were] before you, and the land is defiled;)"

Jeremiah 3:9, "And it came to pass through the lightness of her whoredom, that she defiled the land, and committed adultery with stones and with stocks."

Ezekiel 36:17, "Son of man, when the house of Israel dwelt in their own land, they defiled it by their own way and by their doings: their way was before me as the uncleanness of a removed woman."

Jeremiah 2:7, "And I brought you into a plentiful country, to eat the fruit thereof and the goodness thereof; but when ye entered, ye defiled my land, and made mine heritage an abomination."

Possession of cursed things: Another means by which a home can be defiled is through the possession of cursed items, such as idols, occult books, rings, satanic symbols, and so forth. Sacred Scripture gives us a good indication that possessing idols can pollute the land and bring a curse upon it:

Ezekiel 36:18, "Wherefore I poured my fury upon them for the blood that they had shed upon the land, and for their idols wherewith they had polluted it."

Jeremiah 50:38, "A drought is upon her waters; and they shall be dried up: for it is the land of graven images, and they are mad upon their idols."

Demons can actually draw power from nea
objects, such as idols, occult items, satanic
even demonic photos. It is vital to rid a hon
from such items before dedicating it to the
driving out the unclean spirits. The Bible lets us know
clearly that physical items can indeed carry spiritual
value:

*Deuteronomy 7:26, "Neither shalt thou bring an
abomination into thine house, lest thou be a cursed
thing like it: but thou shalt utterly detest it, and thou
shalt utterly abhor it; for it is a cursed thing."*

How do you exorcize a home or land?

The first step to exorcizing a home, building, or
property, is to dispose of any cursed items. If there are
occult books, Ouija boards, crystal balls, new age items,
dream catchers or other items on the premises they must
be removed and burned. The next step is to go through
each room, praying the ritual of exorcism and blessing
each room, dedicating it to the Lord.

Just remember that you, as a priest, have the authority
needed to drive those spirits out.

Exorcism Is A Process

While exorcism can be a one-time event, it can also be a
process. Many times it takes multiple sessions before a
person is completely freed of demonic influence.
Sessions can last up to several hours, depending on the
response of the demons.

ANCIENT ORTHODOX RITUAL OF EXORCISM

INTRODUCTORY REMARKS

The exorcist should wear an alb and a purple stole during the prayers of the ritual of exorcism. After making the sign of the cross over the victim, place the ends of the stole on this person's neck.

One may have two normal sized stoles sewn together in order to have a very long stole to extend from the priest to the victim's neck. It is truly amazing how the blessed stole calms and controls the possessed person. Certainly one initially may encounter violent reactions, but that is to be expected. The stole not only symbolizes, but demonstrates the power of the priesthood. Jesus binds the evil spirits with the use of this sacramental.

The priest should also place his right hand on the head of the vicitm. Of course, the imposition of hands was used by Jesus to heal the sick. The church imitates this use in the Sacrament of the Sick and in other ways. Christ blessed children in this way. It has been noted by many individuals that hands of the priest's calm or burn them. If an assistant priest is present, they also may place hands on the person's head. A Bible containing both the Old and New Testaments should be on hand when questioning and commanding the demons to respond. After invoking the Holy Spirit, there is surprising response and confirmation, which are keys to opening up and freeing the person. The Rite of Exorcism uses passages from Jn. 1:1-14; Mk. 16:15-18; Lk. 1:17-20; Lk. 11:14-22; also use what ever passage the Holy Spirit inspires. This can hasten along deliverance and yield many crucial answers to the puzzle.

Although the Blessed Sacrament is the Body and Blood of Jesus, True God and True Man, and not any mere sacramental, it is an excellent practice to use it to bless the sick and possessed. The Blessed Sacrament should not be placed on the head or any other part of the body of the possessed persons, due to the possibility of desecration. This rule or admonition need not apply in those cases where there is no danger or irreverence, that is cases in which the person's actions are nonviolent.

It is truly astounding to observe how many days (when proper use of the Blessed Sacrament is applied to the body of the possessed), can be taken off the whole length of time needed to dislodge the demons. It shortens the process. It may be wise in other cases for the priest himself to carry around his neck the Blessed Sacrament in a Pyx. This may prove at times, necessary for protection.

Then there is the crucifix, which should always be present. The victim will often stare at the cross and be forced to look away. The cross is symbolic of the defeat of Satan through the death of Christ. The long prayer for Solemn Blessing of the Crucifix, "Ut quóties triúmphum divínae humnilitátis, quae supérbiam nostri hostis dejecit" and (how often the divine humility has triumphed casting out the pride of our enemy). "Dignáre respícere, bene + dícere et Sancti + ficáre hanc creaturm incensi, ut omnes languores, omnesque imfirmitates, atque insidiar inimici, odorem ejus sentientes, efffugiant, et separatur a plasmate tuo; ut num quam lædatur amorsu antiqui serpentes" (Deign to care for bless and sanctify those being inflamed by passion and weakness, any sickness, deceits of the foe and suspicious resentments felt by them. Be cast out and driven away from your creature) and "Numquam lædatur a morsu antiqui derpentis" (Never to be hurt by the bite of the ancient serpent).

Basic Rules

The priest who with the particular and explicit permission of his Bishop is about to exorcise those tormented by a demonic entity, must have the necessary piety, prudence and personal integrity. He should perform this most heroic work humbly and courageously, not relying on his own strength, but on the power of God; and he must have no greed for material benefit. Besides, he should be of mature age and be respected as a virtuous person.

Let the exorcist note for himself the tricks and deceits which evil spirits use in order to lead him astray. For they are accustomed to answering falsely. They manifest themselves only under pressure--in the hope that the exorcist will get tired and desist from pressuring them. Or they make it appear that the subject of Exorcism is not possessed at all.

Sometimes, a demon betrays its presence, and then goes into hiding. It appears to have left the body of the possessed free from all molestation, so that the possessed thinks he is completely rid of it. But the exorcist should not, for all that, desist until he sees the signs of liberation.

The Exorcist must remember, therefore, that Our Lord said there is a species of Evil Spirit which cannot be expelled except by prayer and fasting. Let him make sure that he and others follow the example of the Holy Fathers and make use of these two principal means of obtaining divine help and of repelling Evil Spirit.

During Exorcism, the exorcist should use the words of the Bible rather than his own or somebody else's. Also, he should command

Evil Spirit to state whether it is kept within the possessed because of some magical spell or sorcerer's symbol or some occult documents. For the exorcism to succeed, the possessed must surrender them. If he has swallowed something like that, he will vomit it up. If it is outside his body in some place or other, Evil Spirit must tell the exorcist where it is. When the exorcist finds it, he must burn it.

In order for Satan to be driven out of the possessed, the exorcist must be humble. He must rely on God and only God for his answers and direction. Sometimes God forces the demon inside the possessed to reveal truths. However, the exorcist must be careful not to believe all that the demon possessing the victim might say. The demon will reveal exactly what the exorcist wants to hear even though it is not the truth, in order to side track him. The exorcist, out of his own curiosity, should not ask questions to the possessed regarding matters other than the exorcism at hand. Only through much prayer, fasting and humility of the exorcist along with the willingness of the victim, and of course, the grace and Will of God, can one be freed of this affliction.

THE RITUAL OF EXORCISM OF A PERSON

INVOCATION

The invocations are recited by the priest; the responses by all.

P: Lord, have mercy.
All: Lord, have mercy.

P: Christ, have mercy.
All: Christ, have mercy.

P: Lord, have mercy.
All: Lord, have mercy.

P: Christ, hear us.
All: Christ, graciously hear us.

P: God, the Father in heaven.
All: Have mercy on us.

P: God, the Son, Redeemer of the world.
All: Have mercy on us.

P: God, the Holy Spirit.
All: Have mercy on us.

P: Holy Trinity, one God.
All: Have mercy on us.

(After each invocation, "Intercede for us.")

P: We ask you Almighty Father to send the Holy Angels to surround us, to bless us, protect us, and to assist us in battle against the Adversary.

All: Intercede for us.

P: We ask Almighty Father for strength, resolve and annointing in this task of delivering your creation from the tortures of the Adversary.

All: Intercede for us.

After each invocation: "Deliver us, 0 Lord."

Priest:

From all sin,
From your wrath,
From sudden and unprovided death,
From the snares of the Devil,
From anger, hatred, and all ill will,
From all lewdness,
From lightning and tempest,
From the scourge of earthquakes,
From plague, famine, and war,
From everlasting death,
By the mystery of your holy incarnation,
By your coming,
By your birth,
By your baptism and holy fasting,
By your cross and passion,
By your death and burial,
By your holy resurrection,
By your wondrous ascension,
By the coming of the Holy,
Spirit, the Advocate,
On the day of judgment,

P: We sinners,
All: We beg you to hear us.

That you spare us,
That you pardon us,
That you bring us to true
penance,
That you govern and preserve
your holy Church,
That you preserve our Holy
Father and all ranks in the
Church in holy religion,

That you humble the enemies
of holy Church,
That you give peace and true
concord to all Christian rulers.
That you give peace and unity
to the whole Christian world,
That you restore to the unity of
the Church all who have
strayed from the truth, and
lead all unbelievers to the light
of the Gospel,

That you confirm and preserve
us in your holy service,
That you lift up our minds to
heavenly desires,
That you grant everlasting
blessings to all our
benefactors,
That you deliver our souls and
the souls of our brethren,
relatives, and benefactors from

everlasting damnation,

That you give and preserve the fruits of the earth,
That you grant eternal rest to all the faithful departed,
That you graciously hear us, Son of God,

P: *Antiphon:* Do not keep in mind, 0 Lord, our offenses or those of our parents, nor take vengeance on our sins.

P: Our Father, who art in heaven, hallowed be thy name. Thy kingdom come, thy will be done, on earth as it is in heaven. Give us this day our daily bread, and forgive us our trespasses, as we forgive those who trespass againts us.And lead us not into temptation.
All: But deliver us from evil. Amen.

Psalm 53

P: God, by your name save me, and by your might defend my cause.
All: God, hear my prayer; hearken to the words of my mouth.

P: For haughty men have risen up against me, and fierce men seek my life; they set not God before their eyes.

All: See, God is my helper; the Lord sustains my life.

P: Turn back the evil upon my foes; in your faithfulness destroy them.
All: Freely will I offer you sacrifice; I will praise your name, Lord, for its goodness,

P: Because from all distress you have rescued me, and my eyes look down upon my enemies.

All: Glory be to the Father, to the Son, and to the Holy Spirit; as it was in th ebeginning, is now and ever shall be, world without end. Amen.

P: Save your servant.
All: Who trusts in you, my God.

P: Let him (her) find in you, Lord, a fortified tower.
All: In the face of the enemy.

P: Let the enemy have no power over him (her).
All: And the son of iniquity be powerless to harm him (her).

P: Lord, send him (her) aid from your holy place.
All: And watch over him (her) from

Sion.

P: Lord, heed my prayer.
All: And let my cry be heard by you.

P: The Lord be with you.
All: May He also be with you.

P: Let us pray.
God, whose nature is ever merciful and forgiving, accept our prayer that this servant of yours, bound by the fetters of sin, may be pardoned by your loving kindness.

Holy Lord, almighty Father, everlasting God and Father of our Lord Jesus Christ, who once and for all consigned that fallen and apostate tyrant to the flames of hell, who sent your only-begotten Son into the world to crush that roaring lion; hasten to our call for help and snatch from ruination and from the clutches of the noonday devil this human being made in your image and likeness. Strike terror, Lord, into the beast now laying waste your vineyard. Fill your servants with courage to fight manfully against that reprobate dragon, lest he despise those who put their trust in you, and say with Pharaoh of old: "I know not God, nor will I set Israel free." Let your mighty hand cast him out of

your servant, **N.**, ✠so he may no longer hold captive this person whom it pleased you to make in your image, and to redeem through your Son; who lives and reigns with you, in the unity of the Holy Spirit, God, forever and ever.
All: Amen.

The Priest commands the demon as follows:

I command you, unclean spirit, whoever you are, along with all your minions now attacking this servant of God, be they demons, Nephilim, Watchers, or unclean spirits, by the mysteries of the incarnation, passion, resurrection, and ascension of our Lord Jesus Christ, by the descent of the Holy Spirit, by the coming of our Lord for judgment, that you tell me by some sign your name, and the day and hour of your departure. I command you, moreover, to obey me to the letter, I who am a priest of God despite my unworthiness; nor shall you be emboldened to harm in any way this creature of God, or the bystanders, or any of their possessions.

The priest lays his hand on the head

of the sick person, saying:

They shall lay their hands upon the sick and all will be well with them. May Jesus, Son of Mary, Lord and Saviour of the world, show you favour and mercy.
All: Amen.

Next he reads over the possessed person these selections from the Gospel.

P: The Lord be with you.
All: May He also be with you.

P: The beginning of the holy Gospel according to St. John.
All: Glory be to you, 0 Lord.

A Lesson from the holy Gospel according to St. John

John 1.1-14

As he says these opening words he signs himself and the possessed on the brow, lips, and breast.

When time began, the Word was there, and the Word was face to face with God, and the Word was God. This Word, when time began, was face to face with God. All things came into being through Him, and without Him there came to be not one thing that has come to be. In Him was life, and the life was the light of men. The light shines in the darkness, and the darkness did not lay hold of it. There came upon the scene a man, a messenger from God, whose name was John. This man came to give testimony to testify in behalf of the light that all might believe through him. He was not himself the light; he only was to testify in behalf of the light. Meanwhile the true light, which illumines every man, was making its entrance into the world. He was in the world, and the world came to be through Him, and the world did not acknowledge Him. He came into His home, and His own people did not welcome Him. But to as many as welcomed Him He gave the power to become children of God those who believe in His name; who were born not of blood, or of carnal desire, or of man's will; no, they were born of God. (Genuflect here.) And the Word became man and lived among us; and we have looked upon His glory such a glory as befits the Father's only-begotten Son full of grace and truth!

All: Thanks be to God.

Lastly he blesses the afflicted person, saying:

May the blessing of almighty God, Father, Son, ✠and Holy Spirit, come upon you and remain with you forever.
All: Amen.

Then he sprinkles the person with holy water.

A Lesson from the holy Gospel according to St. Mark

Mark 16.15-18

At that time Jesus said to His disciples: "Go into the whole world and preach the Gospel to all creation. He that believes and is baptized will be saved; he that does not believe will be condemned. And in the way of proofs of their claims, the following will accompany those who believe: in my name they will drive out demons; they will speak in new tongues; they will take up serpents in their hands, and if they drink something deadly, it will not hurt them; they will lay their hands on the sick, and these will recover."

A Lesson from the holy Gospel according to St. Luke

Luke 10.17-20

At that time the seventy-two returned in high spirits. "Master," they said, "even the demons are subject to us because we use your name!" "Yes," He said to them, "I was watching Satan fall like lightning that flashes from heaven. But mind: it is I that have given you the power to tread upon serpents and scorpions, and break the dominion of the enemy everywhere; nothing at all can injure you. Just the same, do not rejoice in the fact that the spirits are subject to you, but rejoice in the fact that your names are engraved in heaven."

A Lesson from the holy Gospel according to St. Luke

Luke 11.14-22

At that time Jesus was driving out a demon, and this particular demon was dumb. The demon was driven out, the dumb man spoke, and the crowds were enraptured. But some among the people remarked: "He is a tool of Beelzebul, and that is how he drives out demons!" Another group, intending to test Him, demanded of Him a proof of His claims, to be shown in the sky. He knew their inmost thoughts. "Any kingdom torn by civil strife," He said to them, "is laid in ruins; and house tumbles upon house. So, too, if Satan is in revolt against himself, how can his kingdom last, since you say that I drive out demons as a tool of Beelzebul. And furthermore: if I drive out demons as a tool of Beelzebul, whose tools are your pupils when they do the driving out? Therefore, judged by them, you must stand condemned. But, if, on the contrary, I drive out demons by the finger of God, then, evidently the kingdom of God has by this time made its way to you. As long as a mighty lord in full armour guards his premises, he is in peaceful possession of his property; but should one mightier than he attack and overcome him, he will strip him of his armour, on which he had relied, and distribute the spoils taken from him."

P: Lord, heed my prayer.
All: And let my cry be heard by you.

P: The Lord be with you.
All: May He also be with you.

Let us pray.
Almighty Lord, Word of God the

Father, Jesus Christ, God and Lord of all creation; who gave to your holy apostles the power to tramp underfoot serpents and scorpions; who along with the other mandates to work miracles was pleased to grant them the authority to say: "Depart, you demons!" and by whose might Satan was made to fall from heaven like lightning; I humbly call on your holy name in fear and trembling, asking that you grant me, your unworthy servant, pardon for all my sins, steadfast faith, and the power — supported by your mighty arm — to confront with confidence and resolution this cruel demon. I ask this through you, Jesus Christ, our Lord and God, who are coming to judge both the living and the dead and the world by fire.
All: Amen.

Next he makes the sign of the cross over himself and the one possessed, places the end of the stole on the latter's neck, and, putting his right hand on the latter's head, he says the following filled with confidence and faith:

P: See the cross of the Lord; begone, you hostile powers!

All: The stem of David, the lion of Judah's tribe has conquered.

P: Lord, heed my prayer.
All: And let my cry be heard by you.

P: The Lord be with you.
All: May He also be with you.

Let us pray.
God and Father of our Lord Jesus Christ, I appeal to your holy name, humbly begging your kindness, that you graciously grant me help against this and every unclean spirit now tormenting this creature of yours; through Christ our Lord.
All: Amen.

Exorcism

I cast you out, unclean spirit, along with every Satanic power of the enemy, every spectre from hell, every demon, unclean spirit, Nephilim, Watcher, and all your fell companions; in the name of our Lord Jesus ✠Christ. Begone and stay far from this creature of God. ✠For it is He who commands you, He who flung you headlong from the heights of heaven into the depths of hell. It is He who commands you, He who once stilled the sea and the wind and the storm. Hearken, therefore, and tremble in fear, Satan, you enemy of the faith, you foe of the human race, you begetter of death, you robber of life, you corrupter of justice, you root of all evil and vice; seducer of men, betrayer of the nations, instigator of envy, font of avarice, fomenter of discord, author of pain and sorrow. Why, then, do you stand and resist, knowing as you must that Christ the Lord brings your plans to nothing? Fear Him, who in Isaac was offered in sacrifice, in Joseph sold into bondage, slain as the paschal lamb, crucified as man, yet triumphed over the powers of hell. (The three signs of the cross which follow are traced on the brow of the possessed person). Begone, then, in the name of the Father, ✠and of the Son, ✠and of the Holy ✠Spirit. Give place to the Holy Spirit by this sign of the holy ✠cross of our Lord Jesus Christ, who lives and reigns with the Father and the Holy Spirit, God, forever and ever. All: Amen.

P: Lord, heed my prayer.
All: And let my cry be heard by you.

P: The Lord be with you.
All: May He also be with you.

Let us pray.
God, Creator and defender of the human race, who made man in your

own image, look down in pity on this your servant, **N.**, now in the toils of the unclean spirit, now caught up in the fearsome threats of man's ancient enemy, sworn foe of our race, who befuddles and stupefies the human mind, throws it into terror, overwhelms it with fear and panic. Repel, 0 Lord, the Devil's power, break asunder his snares and traps, put the unholy tempter to flight. By the sign ✠ *(on the brow)* of your name, let your servant be protected in mind and body. *(The three crosses which follow are traced on the breast of the possessed person).* Keep watch over the inmost recesses of his (her) ✠heart; rule over his (her) ✠emotions; strengthen his (her) ✠will. Let vanish from his (her) soul the temptings of the mighty adversary. Graciously grant, 0 Lord, as we call on your holy name, that the evil spirit, who hitherto terrorized over us, may himself retreat in terror and defeat, so that this servant of yours may sincerely and steadfastly render you the service which is your due; through Christ our Lord.
All: Amen

I adjure you, ancient serpent, by the judge of the living and the dead, by your Creator, by the Creator of the whole universe, by Him who has the power to consign you to hell, to depart forthwith in fear, along with your savage minions, from this servant of God, **N.**, who seeks refuge in the fold of the Church. I adjure you again, ✠ **(on the brow)** not by my weakness but by the might of the Holy Spirit, to depart from this servant of God, **N.** , whom almighty God has made in His image. Yield, therefore, yield not to my own person but to the minister of Christ. For it is the power of Christ that compels you, who brought you low by His cross. Tremble before that mighty arm that broke asunder the dark prison walls and led souls forth to light. May the trembling that afflicts this human frame, ✠ **(on the breast)** the fear that afflicts this image ✠ **(on the brow)** of God, descend on you. Make no resistance nor delay in departing from this man, for it has pleased Christ to dwell in man. Do not think of despising my command because you know me to be a great sinner. It is God ✠Himself who commands you; the majestic Christ ✠who commands you. God the Father ✠commands you; God the Son ✠commands you; God the Holy

✠Spirit commands you. The mystery of the cross commands ✠you. The faith of the holy apostles Peter and Paul and of all the saints commands ✠you. The blood of the martyrs commands ✠you. The continence of the confessors commands ✠you. The devout prayers of all holy men and women command ✠you. The saving mysteries of our Christian faith command ✠you.

Depart, then, transgressor. Depart, seducer, full of lies and cunning, foe of virtue, persecutor of the innocent. Give place, abominable creature, give way, you monster, give way to Christ, in whom you found none of your works. For He has already stripped you of your powers and laid waste your kingdom, bound you prisoner and plundered your weapons. He has cast you forth into the outer darkness, where everlasting ruin awaits you and your abettors. To what purpose do you insolently resist? To what purpose do you brazenly refuse? For you are guilty before almighty God, whose laws you have transgressed. You are guilty before His Son, our Lord Jesus Christ, whom you presumed to tempt, whom you dared to nail to the cross. You are guilty before the whole human race, to whom you proferred by your enticements the poisoned cup of death.

Therefore, I adjure you, profligate dragon, in the name of the spotless ✠Lamb, who has trodden down the asp and the basilisk, and overcome the lion and the dragon, to depart from this man (woman) (on the brow), to depart from the Church of God ✠ (signing the bystanders). Tremble and flee, as we call on the name of the Lord, before whom the denizens of hell cower, to whom the heavenly Virtues and Powers and Dominations are subject, whom the Cherubim and Seraphim praise with unending cries as they sing: Holy, holy, holy, Lord God of Sabaoth. The Word made flesh ✠commands you; the Virgin's Son ✠commands you; Jesus ✠of Nazareth commands you, who once, when you despised His disciples, forced you to flee in shameful defeat from a man; and when He had cast you out you did not even dare, except by His leave, to enter into a herd of swine. And now as I adjure you in His ✠name, begone from this man (woman) who is His creature. It is futile to resist

His ✠will. It is hard for you to kick against the ✠goad. The longer you delay, the heavier your punishment shall be; for it is not men you are condemning, but rather Him who rules the living and the dead, who is coming to judge both the living and the dead and the world by fire.
All: Amen.

P: Lord, heed my prayer.
All: And let my cry be heard by you.

P: The Lord be with you.
All: May He also be with you.

Let us pray.
God of heaven and earth, God of the angels and archangels, God of the prophets and apostles, God of the martyrs and virgins, God who have power to bestow life after death and rest after toil; for there is no other God than you, nor can there be another true God beside you, the Creator of heaven and earth, who are truly a King, whose kingdom is without end; I humbly entreat your glorious majesty to deliver this servant of yours from the unclean spirits; through Christ our Lord.
All: Amen.

Therefore, I adjure you every unclean spirit, every spectre from hell, every satanic power, in the name of Jesus ✠Christ of Nazareth, who was led into the desert after His baptism by John to vanquish you in your citadel, to cease your assaults against the creature whom He has, formed from the slime of the earth for His own honor and glory; to quail before wretched man, seeing in him the image of almighty God, rather than his state of human frailty. Yield then to God, ✠who by His servant, Moses, cast you and your malice, in the person of Pharaoh and his army, into the depths of the sea. Yield to God, ✠who, by the singing of holy canticles on the part of David, His faithful servant, banished you from the heart of King Saul. Yield to God, ✠who condemned you in the person of Judas Iscariot, the traitor. For He now flails you with His divine scourges, ✠He in whose sight you and your legions once cried out: "What have we to do with you, Jesus, Son of the Most High God? Have you come to torture us before the time?" Now He is driving you back into the everlasting fire, He who at the end of time will say to the wicked: "Depart from me, you accursed, into the everlasting fire which has been prepared for the devil and his angels." For you, 0 evil one, and for your followers there will be worms that never die. An unquenchable fire stands ready for you and for your minions, you prince of accursed murderers, father of lechery, instigator of sacrileges, model of vileness, promoter of heresies, inventor of every obscenity.

Depart, then, ✠impious one, depart, ✠accursed one, depart with all your deceits, for God has willed that man should be His temple. Why do you still linger here? Give honour to God the Father ✠almighty, before whom every knee must bow. Give place to the Lord Jesus ✠Christ, who shed His most precious blood for man. Give place to the Holy ✠Spirit, who by His blessed apostle Peter openly struck you down in the person of Simon Magus; who cursed your lies in Annas and Saphira; who smote you in King Herod because he had not given honor to God; who by His apostle Paul afflicted you with the night of blindness in the magician Elyma, and by the mouth of the same apostle bade you to go out of Pythonissa, the soothsayer. Begone, ✠now! Begone, ✠seducer! Your place is in solitude; your abode is in the nest of serpents; get down and crawl with them. This matter brooks no delay; for see, the Lord, the ruler comes quickly, kindling fire before Him, and it will run on ahead of Him and encompass His enemies in flames. You might delude man, but God you cannot mock. It is He who casts you out, from whose sight nothing is hidden. It is He who repels you, to whose might all things are subject. It is He who expels you, He who has prepared everlasting hellfire for you and your angels, from whose mouth shall come a sharp sword, who is coming to judge both the living and the dead and the world by fire.

All: Amen.

Exorcism Prayers of St. John Chrysostom

P: O Eternal God, Who has redeemed the race of men from the captivity of the devil, deliver Thy servant/handmaid from all the workings of unclean spirits. Command the evil and impure spirits and demons to depart from the soul and body of your servant/handmaid and not to remain nor hide in him/her. Let them be banished from this the creation of Thy hands in

Thine own holy name and that of
Thine only begotten Son and of Thy
life-creating Spirit, so that, after
being cleansed from all demonic
influence, he/she may live godly,
justly and righteously and may be
counted worthy to receive the Holy
Mysteries of Thine only-begotten
Son and our God with Whom Thou
art blessed and glorified together
with the all holy and good and life-
creating Spirit now and ever and
unto the ages of ages. Amen.

All: O Thou Who hast rebuked all
unclean spirits and by the power of
Thy Word has banished the legion,
come now, through Thine only
begotten Son upon this creature,
which Thou hast fashioned in Thine
own image and deliver him/her from
the adversary that holds him/her in
bondage, so that, receiving Thy
mercy and becoming purified, he/she
might join the ranks of Thy holy
flock and be preserved as a living
temple of the Holy Spirit and might
receive the divine and holy Mysteries
through the grace and compassion
and loving kindness of Thine only-
begotten Son with Whom Thou art
blessed together with Thine all-holy

and good and life-creating Spirit now and ever and unto the ages of ages. Amen.

P: We beseech Thee, O Lord, Almighty God, Most High, untempted, peaceful King. We beseech Thee Who has created the heaven and the earth, for out of Thee has issued the Alpha and the Omega, the beginning and the end, Thou Who has ordained that the fourfooted and irrational beasts be under subjection to man, for Thou hast subjected them. Lord, stretch out Thy mighty hand and Thy sublime and holy arm and in Thy watchful care look down upon this Thy creature and send down upon him/her a peaceful angel, a mighty angel, a guardian of soul and body, that will rebuke and drive away every evil and unclean demon from him/her, for Thou alone are Lord, Most High, almighty and blessed unto ages of ages. Amen.

All: We make this great, divine, holy and awesome invocation and plea, O devil, for thine expulsion, as well as this rebuke for your utter annihilation, O apostate! God Who is holy, beginningless, frightful, invisible in essence, infinite in power and incomprehensible in divinity, the King of glory and Lord Almighty, He shall rebuke thee, devil! -- He Who composed all things well by his Word from nothingness into being; He Who walks upon the wings of the air. The Lord rebukes thee, devil! -- He Who calls forth the water of the sea and pours it upon the face of all the earth. Lord of Hosts is His name.

P: Devil: the Lord rebukes thee! He Who is ministered to and praised by numberless heavenly orders and adored and glorified in fear by multitudes of angelic and archangelic hosts. Satan: the Lord rebukes thee! He Who is honored by the encircling Powers, the awesome six-winged and many-eyed Cherubim and Seraphim that cover their faces with two wings because of His inscrutable and unseen divinity and with two wings cover their feet, lest they be seared by His unutterable glory and incomprehensible majesty, and with two wings do fly and fill the heavens with their shouts of "Holy, holy, holy, Lord Sabaoth, heaven and earth are full of Thy glory!" Devil: The Lord rebukes thee! He Who came down from the Father's bosom and, through the holy, inexpressible, immaculate and adorable Incarnation from the Virgin, appeared ineffably in the world to save it and cast thee down from heaven in His authoritative power and showed thee to be an outcast to every man. Satan: The Lord rebukes thee! He Who said to the sea, be silent, be still, and instantly it was calmed at His command. Devil: The Lord rebukes thee! He Who made clay with His immaculate spittle and refashioned the wanting member of the man blind from birth and gave him his sight. Devil: The Lord rebukes thee! He Who by His word restored to life the daughter of the ruler of the synagogue and snatched the son of the widow out from the mouth of death and gave him whole and sound to his own mother. Devil: The Lord rebukes thee! The Lord Who raised Lazarus the four-days dead from the dead, undecayed, as if not having died, and unblemished to the astonishment of many. Satan: The Lord rebukes thee! He Who destroyed the curse by the blow on His face and by the lance in His immaculate side lifted the flaming sword that guarded Paradise. Devil: The Lord rebukes thee! He Who dried all tears from every face by the spitting upon His precious expressed image. Devil: The Lord rebukes thee! He Who set His Cross as a support, the salvation of the world, to thy fall and the fall of all the angels under thee. Devil: The Lord rebukes thee! He Who spoke from His Cross and the curtain of the temple was torn in two, and the rocks were split and the tombs were opened and those who were dead from the ages were raised up. Devil: The Lord rebukes thee! He Who by death put death to death and by His rising granted life to all men. May the Lord rebuke thee, Satan! -- that is, He Who descended into Hades and opened its tombs and set free those held prisoner in it, calling them to Himself; before Whom the gatekeepers of Hades shuddered when they saw Him and, hiding themselves, vanished in the anguish of Hades. May the Lord rebuke thee, devil! -- That is, Christ our God Who arose from the dead and granted His Resurrection to all men. May the Lord rebuke thee, Satan! -- He Who in glory ascended into heaven to His Father, sitting on the right of majesty upon the throne of glory. Devil: May the Lord rebuke thee! He Who shall come again with glory upon the clouds of heaven with His holy angels to judge the living and the dead. Devil: May the Lord rebuke thee! He Who has prepared for thee unquenchable fire, the unsleeping worm and the outer darkness unto eternal punishment. Devil: May the Lord rebuke thee! For before Him all things shudder and tremble from the face of His power and the wrath of His warning upon thee is uncontainable. Satan: The Lord rebukes thee by His frightful name! Shudder, tremble, be afraid, depart, be utterly destroyed, be banished! Thee who fell from heaven and together with thee all evil spirits: every evil spirit of lust, the spirit of evil, a day and nocturnal spirit, a noonday and evening spirit, a midnight spirit, an imaginative spirit, an encountering spirit, either of the dry land or of the water, or one in a forest, or among the reeds, or in trenches, or in a road or a crossroad, in lakes, or streams, in houses, or one sprinkling in the baths and chambers, or one altering the mind of man. Depart swiftly from this creature of the Creator Christ our God! And be gone from the servant/handmaid of God _____, from his/her mind, from his/her soul, from his/her heart, from his/her reins, from his/her senses, from all his/her members, that he/she might become whole and sound and free, knowing God, his/her own Master and Creator of all things, He Who gathers together those who have gone astray and Who gives them the seal of salvation through the rebirth andrestoration of divine Baptism, so that he may be counted worthy of His immaculate, heavenly and awesome Mysteries and be united to His true fold, dwelling in a place of pasture and nourished on the waters of repose, guided pastorally and safely by the staff of the Cross unto the forgiveness of sins and life everlasting. For unto Him belong all glory, honor, adoration and majesty together with Thy beginningless Father and His all-holy, good and life-giving Spirit, now and ever, and unto ages of ages.

All: Amen.

P: Antiphon: Magi from the East came to Bethlehem to adore the Lord; and opening their treasure chests they presented Him with precious gifts: Gold for the great King, incense for the true God, and myrrh in symbol of His burial. Alleluia.

Canticle of Our Lady (The Magnificat)
Luke 1:46 55

P: "My soul extols the Lord;
All: And my spirit leaps for joy in
God my Saviour.

P: How graciously He looked upon
His lowly maid! Oh, see, from this
hour onward age after age will call
me blessed!

All: How sublime is what He has
done for me, the Mighty One, whose
name is `Holy'!
P: From age to age He visits those
who worship Him in reverence.
All: His arm achieves the mastery:
He routs the haughty and proud of
heart.

P: He puts down princes from their
thrones, and exalts the lowly;
All: He fills the hungry with
blessings, and sends away the rich
with empty hands.

P: He has taken by the hand His
servant Israel, and mercifully kept
His faith,
All: As He had promised our fathers
with Abraham and his posterity
forever and evermore."

P: Glory be to the Father, etc.
All: As it was in the beginning, etc.

Antiphon: Magi from the East came to Bethlehem to adore the Lord; and opening their treasure chests they presented Him with precious gifts: Gold for the great King, incense for the true God, and myrrh in symbol of His burial. Alleluia.

Meanwhile the home is sprinkled with holy water and incensed. Then the priest says:

P: Our Father *(the rest inaudibly until:)*

P: And lead us not into temptation.
All: But deliver us from evil.

P: Many shall come from Saba.
All: Bearing gold and incense.

P: Lord, heed my prayer.
All: And let my cry be heard by you.

P: The Lord be with you.
All: May he also be with you.

Let us pray.
God, who on this day revealed your only-begotten Son to all nations by the guidance of a star, grant that we who now know you by faith may finally behold you in your heavenly majesty; through Christ our Lord.
All: Amen.

Responsory: Be enlightened and shine forth, 0 Jerusalem, for your light is come; and upon you is risen the glory of the Lord Jesus Christ born of the Virgin Mary.

P: Nations shall walk in your light, and kings in the splendour of your birth.
All: And the glory of the Lord is risen upon you.

Let us pray.
Lord God almighty, bless ✠this home, and under its shelter let there be health, chastity, self-conquest, humility, goodness, mildness, obedience to your commandments, and thanksgiving to God the Father, Son, and Holy Spirit. May your blessing remain always in this home and on those who live here; through Christ our Lord.
All: Amen.

P: **Antiphon for Canticle of Zachary:**
Today the Church is espoused to her heavenly bridegroom, for Christ washes her sins in the Jordan; the Magi hasten with gifts to the regal nuptials; and the guests are gladdened with water made wine,alleluia.

Canticle of Zachary
Luke 1:68 79

P: "Blessed be the Lord, the God of Israel! He has visited His people and brought about its redemption.

All: He has raised for us a stronghold of salvation in the house of David His servant,
P: And redeemed the promise He had made through the mouth of His holy prophets of old

All: To grant salvation from our foes and from the hand of all that hate us;
P: To deal in mercy with our fathers and be mindful of His holy covenant,

All: Of the oath he had sworn to our father Abraham, that He would enable us

P: Rescued from the clutches of our foes to worship Him without fear,
All: In holiness and observance of the Law, in His presence, all our days.

P: And you, my little one, will be hailed `Prophet of the Most High'; for the Lord's precursor you will be to prepare His ways;

All: You are to impart to His people knowledge of salvation through forgiveness of their sins.
P: Thanks be to the merciful heart of our God! A dawning Light from on

high will visit us

All: To shine upon those who sit in darkness and in the shadowland of death, and guide our feet into the path of peace."
P: Glory be to the Father., etc.
All: As it was in the beginning, etc.

Antiphon:
Today the Church is espoused to her heavenly bridegroom, for Christ washes her sins in the Jordan; the Magi hasten with gifts to the regal nuptials; and the guests are gladdened with water made wine, alleluia.
P: The Lord be with you.
All: May He also be with you.

Let us pray.
God, who on this day revealed your only-begotten Son to all nations by the guidance of a star, grant that we who now know you by faith may finally behold you in your heavenly majesty; through Christ our Lord.
All: Amen.

Athanasian Creed

P: Whoever wills to be saved must before all else hold fast to the catholic faith.
All: Unless one keeps this faith

whole and untarnished, without doubt he will perish forever.

P: Now this is the catholic faith: that we worship one God in Trinity, and Trinity in unity;
All: Neither confusing the Persons one with the other, nor making a distinction in their nature.

P: For the Father is a distinct Person; and so is the Son; and so is the Holy Spirit.
All: Yet the Father, Son, and Holy Spirit possess one Godhead, co-equal glory, co-eternal majesty.

P: As the Father is, so is the Son, so also is the Holy Spirit.
All: The Father is uncreated, the Son is uncreated, the Holy Spirit is uncreated.

P: The Father is infinite, the Son is infinite, the Holy Spirit is infinite.
All: The Father is eternal, the Son is eternal, the Holy Spirit is eternal.

P: Yet they are not three eternals, but one eternal God.
All: Even as they are not three uncreated, or three infinites, but one uncreated and one infinite God.

P: So likewise the Father is almighty, the Son is almighty, the

Holy Spirit is almighty.
All: Yet they are not three almighties,
but they are the one Almighty.

P: Thus the Father is God, the Son is
God, the Holy Spirit is God.
All: Yet they are not three gods, but
one God.

P: Thus the Father is Lord, the Son
is Lord, the Holy Spirit is Lord.
All: Yet there are not three lords, but
one Lord.

P: For just as Christian truth
compels us to profess that each
Person is individually God and Lord,
so does the Catholic religion forbid
us to hold that there are three gods or
lords.
All: The Father was not made by any
power; He was neither created nor
begotten.

P: The Son is from the Father alone,
neither created nor made, but
begotten.
All: The Holy Spirit is from the
Father and the Son, neither made nor
created nor begotten, but He
proceeds.

P: So there is one Father, not three;
one Son, not three; one Holy Spirit,
not three.
All: And in this Trinity one Person is

not earlier or later, nor is one greater or less; but all three Persons are co-eternal and co-equal.

P: In every way, then, as already affirmed, unity in Trinity and Trinity in unity is to be worshiped.
All: Whoever, then, wills to be saved must assent to this doctrine of the Blessed Trinity.

P: But it is necessary for everlasting salvation that one also firmly believe in the incarnation of our Lord Jesus Christ.
All: True faith, then, requires us to believe and profess that our Lord Jesus Christ, the Son of God, is both God and man.

P: He is God, begotten of the substance of the Father from eternity; He is man, born in time of the substance of His Mother.
All: He is perfect God, and perfect man subsisting in a rational soul and a human body.

P: He is equal to the Father in His divine nature, but less than the Father in His human nature as such.
All: And though He is God and man, yet He is the one Christ, not two;

P: One, however, not by any change of divinity into flesh, but by the act

of God assuming a human nature.
All: He is one only, not by a mixture
of substance, but by the oneness of
His Person.

P: For, somewhat as the rational soul
and the body compose one man, so
Christ is one Person who is both God
and man;
All: Who suffered for our salvation,
who descended into hell, who rose
again the third day from the dead;

P: Who ascended into heaven, and
sits at the right hand of God the
Father almighty, from there He shall
come to judge both the living and the
dead.
All: At His coming all men shall rise
again in their bodies, and shall give
an account of their works.

P: And those who have done good
shall enter into everlasting life, but
those who have done evil into
everlasting fire.
All: All this is Catholic faith, and
unless one believes it truly and
firmly one cannot be saved.

P: Glory be to the Father
All: As it was in the beginning.

Here follow a large number of psalms which may be used at the exorcist's discretion but are not a necessary part of the rite. Some of them occur in other parts of the Ritual and are so indicated; the others may be taken from the Psalter. Psalm 90 ; psalm 67; psalm 69; psalm 53; psalm 117; psalm 34; psalm 30; psalm 21; psalm 3; psalm 10; psalm 12.

Prayer Following Deliverance

P: Almighty God, we beg you to keep the evil spirit from further molesting this servant of yours, and to keep him far away, never to return. At your command, 0 Lord, may the goodness and peace of our Lord Jesus Christ, our Redeemer, take possession of this man (woman). May we no longer fear any evil since the Lord is with us; who lives and reigns with you, in the unity of the Holy Spirit, God, forever and ever. All: Amen.

EXORCISM OF A PLACE OR HOME

Ritual of exorcism to combat the power of the evil spirits over a community or locality.

P: In the name of the Father, and of the Son, and of the Holy Spirit. Amen.

P: Heavenly Father, we bessench you to send to our aid the mighty angles of the heavenly army, to defend us in the battle against principalities and powers, against the rulers of the world of darkness and the spirit of wickedness in high places. To come to the rescue of mankind, whom You have made in Your own image and likeness, and purchased from Satan's tyranny at so great a price. Your Holy Church honours their presence here with us. You have entrusted to these angels the task of leading the souls of the redeemed to heavenly blessedness. Lord of peace, cast Satan down under our feet, so as to keep him from further holding man captive and doing harm to Your Church. May Your holy angels O Lord quickly come and lay hold of the beast, the serpent of old, Satan and his demons, casting him in chains into the abyss, so that he can no longer seduce the nations.

All: Amen.

Exorcism

P: In the name of Jesus Christ, our Lord and God, and by the authority residing in our holy ministry, we steadfastly proceed to combat the onslaught of the Adversary.

Psalm 67

> P: God arises; His enemies are scattered,

and those who hate Him
flee before Him.
All: As smoke is driven
away, so are they
driven; as wax melts
before the fire, so the
wicked perish before
God.

P: See the cross of the
Lord; begone, you
hostile powers!
All: The stem of David,
the lion of Juda's tribe
has conquered.

P: May your mercy,
Lord, remain with us
always.

All: For we put our
whole trust in you.

P: We cast you out, every
unclean spirit, every satanic
power, every onslaught of the
infernal adversary, every
legion, every diabolical group
and sect, in the name and by
the power of our Lord Jesus
✠Christ. We command you,
begone and fly far from the
Church of God, from the souls
made by God in His image and
redeemed by the precious
blood of the divine Lamb.

✠No longer dare, cunning serpent, to deceive the human race, to persecute God's Church, to strike God's elect and to sift them as wheat. ✠For the Most High God commands you, ✠He to whom you once proudly presumed yourself equal; He who wills all men to be saved and come to the knowledge of truth. God the Father ✠commands you. God the Son ✠commands you. God the Holy ✠Spirit commands you. Christ, the eternal Word of God made flesh, commands ✠you, who humbled Himself, becoming obedient even unto death, to save our racefrom the perdition wrought by your envy; who founded His Church upon a firm rock, declaring that the gates of hell should never prevail against her, and that He would remain with her all days, even to the end of the world. The sacred mystery of the cross ✠commands you, along with the power of all mysteries of Christian faith. ✠The blood of Christ, ✠commands you.

Therefore, accursed dragon and every diabolical legion, we adjure you by the living ✠God, by the true ✠God, by the holy ✠God, by God, who so loved the world that He gave His only-begotten Son, that whoever believes in Him might not perish but have everlasting life; to cease deluding human creatures and filling them with the poison of everlasting damnation; to desist from harming the Church and hampering her freedom. Begone, Satan, father and master of lies, enemy of man's welfare. Give place to Christ, in whom you found none of your works. Give way to the one, holy, catholic, and apostolic Church, which Christ Himself purchased with His blood. Bow down before God's mighty hand, tremble and flee as we call on the holy and awesome name of Jesus, before whom the denizens of hell cower, to whom the heavenly Virtues and Powers and Dominations are subject, whom the Cherubim and Seraphim praise with unending cries as they sing: Holy, holy, holy, Lord God of Sabaoth.

P: Lord, heed my prayer.
All: And let my cry be heard by

P: The Lord be with you.
All: May He also be with you.

Let us pray.
God of heaven and earth, God of the angels and archangels, God of the patriarchs and prophets, God of the apostles and martyrs, God of the confessors and virgins, God who have power to bestow life after death and rest after toil; for there is no other God than you, nor can there be another true God beside you, the Creator of all things visible and invisible, whose kingdom is without end; we humbly entreat your glorious majesty to deliver us by your might from every influence of the accursed spirits, from their every evil snare and deception, and to keep us from all harm; through Christ our Lord.

All: Amen.

P: From the snares of the Devil.
All: Lord, deliver us.

P: That you help your Church to serve you in security and freedom.
All: We beg you to hear us.

P: That you humble the enemies of holy Church.

All: Amen.

The surroundings are sprinkled with holy water.

Made in the USA
Lexington, KY
21 June 2016